Spotlight on Spelling

A teacher's toolkit of instant spelling activities

Glynis Hannell

Routledge
Taylor & Francis Group

LONDON AND NEW YORK

First published 2009
by Routledge
2 Park Square, Milton Park, Abingdon, Oxon OX14 4RN

Routledge is an imprint of the Taylor & Francis Group, an informa business

© 2009 Glynis Hannell

Typeset in Sabon by
Florence Production Ltd, Stoodleigh, Devon
Printed and bound in Great Britain by
MPG Books Ltd, Bodmin

British Library Cataloguing in Publication Data
A catalogue record for this book is available from the British Library

ISBN10: 0–415–47305–5 (pbk)
ISBN13: 978–0–415–47305–7 (pbk)

Contents

Other books from Routledge by Glynis Hannell

Spotlight on Language: A teacher's toolkit of instant language activities
978–0–415–47311–8

Spotlight on Writing: A teacher's toolkit of instant writing activities
978–0–415–47308–8

Spotlight on Reading: A teacher's toolkit of instant reading activities
978–0–415–47307–1

Spotlight on Your Inclusive Classroom: A teacher's toolkit of instant inclusive activities
978–0–415–47306–4

Success with Inclusion: 1001 Teaching strategies and activities that really work
978–0–415–44534–4

Dyscalculia: Action plans for successful learning in mathematics
978–1–84312–387–3

Dyslexia: Action plans for successful learning
978–1–84312–214–2

Promoting Positive Thinking: Building children's self-esteem, self-confidence and optimism
978–1–84312–257–9

CHAPTER 1

Introduction

Spelling: an important skill

Spelling is an important sub-skill of writing, helping writers to communicate accurately. Although meaning can often be clear despite poor spelling, there are times when perfect spelling is essential. Good spelling helps with writing fluency, good expression and confidence. A well-written letter, email or other communication with good spelling creates a favourable impression of the writer.

Poor spelling skills

Without good skills in written communication pupils cannot fully participate in written exchanges with other people at home, at school and in the community and, in later years, in the workplace. Without good spelling pupils are disadvantaged in many ways. Pupils may:

- restrict what they write to keep within the limits of their spelling ability;

- become disheartened and frustrated by errors that detract from otherwise good pieces of writing;

- work very slowly in an effort to get their spelling correct and in doing so fail to complete tasks;

- experience embarrassment because of ridicule or punishment for spelling errors.

In later years pupils who cannot spell well may:

- hold back from seeking or accepting roles that are likely to expose poor spelling;

- avoid further education, training or promotion if they fear that their spelling skills will let them down;

- feel inadequate in comparison to others who can spell well.

Your inclusive classroom

An effective classroom literacy programme will take into consideration the needs of pupils who may need individualised materials, explicit teaching and opportunities for extended practice to build their skills. An inclusive approach to the teaching of literacy delivers a double advantage to pupils. First, a flexible, inclusive approach will mean that all pupils with receive appropriate teaching and make the best progress possible. Second, the advantages of good spelling skills will filter into every aspect of the pupils' life, at school and beyond.

If classroom instruction fails to be sufficiently inclusive and/or appropriate to the pupils' needs, the pupils' spelling skills will fail to develop and the cycle of disadvantage and negativity increases. However, when success is experienced, confidence, interest, motivation and enjoyment often follow.

Spelling is a complex skill and it follows that many pupils in your classroom will need a high level of effective, inclusive teaching over an extended period of time, in order to be able to reach a reasonable level of competence.

Spelling can be challenging

Many pupils can learn to spell a particular word for a short period of time, but cannot 'hold' the spelling pattern over a longer period of time. Why is this?

Partly, it is because the English language has evolved from several sources, each with a different set of spelling patterns. If a written language does have a single set of regular spelling rules that apply to all words in that language, learning to spell in that language is relatively easy. The young learner needs only to master the one underlying system. They can then apply that system to every word that they wish to spell. In turn, this means that the pupil can fall back on reconstituting a word, according to set principles, when necessary. The pupil does not actually have to learn how to spell *spin*, *nip*, *pin* or *sin*. The same letters and sounds can be successfully recycled as often as needed! Unfortunately, only about 65 per cent of English words fall into this category.

The remaining 35 per cent are irregular, and cannot simply be rebuilt using the standard system. If they could, *one* would be written as *wun*, *Wednesday* as *Wensday* and so on. Instead, these words have to be committed to memory in order for their unexpected spelling patterns to be accurately recalled at a later stage.

Some pupils have difficulties with rote learning and find it very hard to remember the exact spelling of all the irregular or exception words. It is a big task. Just imagine if, instead of recycling the same numbers over and over again when you counted, you had to learn a new word for every single figure from one to one thousand! It would take a lot of effort and constant practice, and I suspect that few of us would fully master the entire set! Learning irregular words places a similar load on memory, and it is not surprising that so many pupils experience difficulty.

Even with a regular system of phonics, some pupils will still experience problems with accurate spelling, because they have problems with phonological awareness (the process of identifying speech sounds in words) or they have insufficient grasp of the letter–sound associations and spelling rules that underpin the spelling of regular words.

Let us look at how this book, *Spotlight on Spelling*, connects with the basic building blocks of spelling and enables you, the teacher, to provide effective, inclusive teaching for all your pupils.

Spotlight on Spelling: foundations of success

Listening for sounds

Pupils are able to spell a wide range of words successfully if they are able to detect and manipulate sounds within words. This skill is called *phonological awareness* and it is a foundation skill that leads to competence in both reading and spelling regular words.

Pupils have to learn to be quite analytical when they listen to a word and break the word into a series of sounds, for example *Does 'goal' start with a 'g' sound or a 'c' sound?* or *Does 'smart' end with a 't' sound or a 'd' sound?*

Once sounds have been identified, spelling can begin. Pupils can either start from scratch and spell a new word, or use another word that they can already spell and simply swap the sounds around.

Chapter 2 offers a range of activities to develop your pupils' phonological awareness.

Letters and sounds

Once pupils have identified the sounds in words, they need to be able to turn those sounds into print. To do this they must use the correct letters for each sound. For example, they must know how two (or more) single letters often make a new sound such as *oa*, *ing*, *ie* and so on, before they can successfully spell words such as *boat*, *sing* or *pie*.

We know that pupils who can use *morphemes* (the smallest units of sound that have meaning) can rapidly expand their spelling repertoire, so the ability to use *prefixes* and *suffixes* is a very useful addition to the pupils' set of skills. This involves not only knowing how to spell the morphemes, but also knowing the rules that govern their use.

Chapter 3 is the chapter that can be used for activities relating to the use of letters to represent sounds.

Tough words

As we all know only too well, English has many irregular or exception words that are *tough* to learn. Unfortunately, many of the words are very commonly used and so really do have to be learned.

However, on the plus side, some of the more interesting words to use also have unusual spelling patterns, so pupils can have fun learning how to spell some obscure words.

Chapter 4 contains the activities that introduce tough words for your pupils to learn. As well as learning how to spell the words your pupils will gain insight in *how* to learn to spell tough words.

Mixed challenges

Spelling is multifaceted and learning to spell well involves many different skills and strategies. First, teachers will need to establish how well their pupils can already spell, and then identify words that are not yet known. Some pupils need quite intensive practice over a number of days to really master the words they are not sure of, whereas others can learn more quickly. All pupils benefit from practising spelling words in context rather than only in a list.

Chapter 5, as well as containing two interesting activities, *Anagrams* and *Twisters*, to engage pupils in some fun-based learning, offers teachers a simple spelling checklist of commonly used words. One activity gives pupils and teachers an opportunity to try out different ways of learning to spell and there are two charts to provide structure for spelling practice.

Effective, inclusive teaching

Let us briefly look at some of the key elements of effective, inclusive teaching:

- Continuous interaction occurs between teacher and pupil, to explore, discuss and deal with the spelling tasks that have been set.

- All pupils can participate in the same type of activity within the classroom, with differentiated learning materials if necessary.

- Pupils of differing spelling abilities can interact and learn from each other.

- Pupils are not excluded from full classroom participation because of stereotypes of what they can and cannot do.

- The spelling activities provided offer a reasonable degree of challenge to encourage new learning to take place.

- Skills are built up through specific activities designed to help pupils really understand the process of spelling.

- Sub-skills of spelling are explicitly taught to enable all pupils to master the skills of phonological awareness, letter–sound associations, spelling rules and spelling irregular words.

- Pupils are provided with spelling activities that match their level of skill and that are designed to promote further development.

- Less able pupils are protected from failure or frustration because they are given appropriate levels of scaffolding and support for the more difficult tasks.

- Less able pupils are given differentiated learning materials that are appropriate to their needs.

- The teacher facilitates learning for each individual pupil in the class, according to their needs.

- Explicit instruction in spelling strategies is used as a key teaching strategy.

- Teachers provide good examples of appropriate responses to help pupils understand the nature of a task.

- Pupils are encouraged to discuss and analyse responses so that they learn to identify and understand what is required.

- Every pupil has sufficient opportunity to practise each sub-skill of spelling until it is mastered.

- Pupils learn to think about their own spelling and learning in a constructive way.

- Mistakes or incorrect answers are viewed as valuable teaching opportunities, used to highlight the general principles of the task.

- Teachers provide spelling activities that engage the pupils' interest.

- Teaching materials provide disadvantaged pupils with enrichment as well as practice in specific skills.

Spotlight on Spelling in your inclusive classroom

Differentiated learning materials for inclusion

Each of the activities is presented at three levels of difficulty. Level 1 is the easiest level, Level 2 intermediate and Level 3 the most difficult. There is deliberate overlap between the three levels to allow for easy transitions between one level and the next.

The gradual increase in difficulty levels and the overlap between levels help teachers to provide *inclusive activities* in their classrooms. One activity can be used to suit a wide range of pupils within a mixed ability class. For example, a teacher may use Level 2 for most of the class, but direct the more able pupils to continue on with Level 3 items, while their younger or less able classmates work on Level 1 items. All pupils will be doing exactly the same activity, but at different levels of difficulty.

Some pupils do need intensive work to master spelling patterns, particularly irregular spellings, and so teachers will obviously differentiate the amount of practice required for individual pupils.

Pupils with language or learning difficulties

Pupils who experience difficulty with language, learning or spelling may benefit from a *differentiated* activity that is on an easier level than the rest of the class. Once the easier level has been completed, the teacher can make a decision on whether to

- provide additional teaching support to help the pupil complete the activity; or

- if the first level is successfully completed, have the pupil progress to the more difficult levels of the same activity; or

- if the first level has only been completed with assistance, have the pupil move to a similar activity, but at the same level of difficulty as before, and provide assistance as required on the new activity.

For example, Bill and Betty have both been given Level 1 of *Change the middle sound* (Activity 5) from Chapter 2, 'Listening for sounds'. Betty coped with this quite easily, so the teacher decides that she can now move on to Levels 2 and 3 of this same activity.

Bill, however, clearly found Level 1 quite challenging, so he is not yet ready for the more difficult Level 2. Instead, the teacher uses Level 1 of *Change the first sound* (Activity 2) as a teaching tool and spends time talking to Bill about each item in turn. The teacher might then return to Level 1 of *Change the middle sound* at a later time.

A key principle for inclusive teaching is that teachers vary the amount and style of *support* given to pupils of varying abilities. For example, while one pupil may be able to answer a question without any prompts or hints, another may need the teacher to give more *scaffolding* and assistance such as:

- discussion

- leading questions

- helpful comments, hints or clues

- multiple choice options.

For example, if Dylan cannot transform the word *dark* into *shark* by just looking at *dark* and then writing down *shark*, his teacher might provide him with letter cards that give him the letters *d-a-r-k-sh-f-k*. The teacher then works with Dylan, first building *dark* and then looking at the letter cards *sh-f-k* to decide which one is needed to replace the *d* in *dark*. The teacher has made the choice very easy for Dylan by giving him two very unlikely letters and the correct letter blend to choose between.

The resultant learning is still valid, but has required more structure to achieve the end result.

Pupils with advanced development

The more advanced pupils often gain considerable insight into a task by participating in the easier items, where the *thinking* processes and the *strategies* used are usually more concrete and overt. For example, in *Spelling tricks* (Activity 21), pupils can analyse their own learning of simple words and apply their preferred strategies to the more difficult words they encounter later.

Pupils who have advanced spelling development usually thrive on activities that challenge them. Teachers can readily select a range of activities and/or levels to provide the bright pupil with *individualised activities* that will extend their spelling skills. For example, a very advanced six-year-old might start with Level 2 of the selected activity and even move through to Level 3 if able to do so.

Interactive, inclusive and explicit teaching

Unlike many other pupil workbooks, *Spotlight on Spelling* activities are intended to be used as *explicit* teaching materials, and as the basis of *interaction* between teacher and pupil(s). Teachers may often find that the younger and less able pupils benefit from participating in classroom *discussion* and attempts at the more difficult levels, classroom interaction and discussion will give them good models for successful completion of the activities. This provides an opportunity for the pupils to be *challenged* and perhaps to break a *stereotype* of what they can and cannot do.

Spelling is a complex skill and many pupils will benefit from working on *sub-skills*, so that small facets of spelling are explicitly taught and practised in a supportive learning environment. Throughout this book, teachers will find activities that focus on a targeted sub-skill of spelling. For example, in *Rules for suffixes* (Activity 11) the pupils, with their teacher's support, work on adding suffixes to words, using a set of rules that can be applied to any word that takes a suffix.

Many of the activities can generate useful discussion and interaction between pupils and teacher (or helping adult) in a small group or one-to-one setting. For example, the activities *Think about spelling (1)* and *(2)* (Activities 14 and 15) offer opportunities for the teacher and pupils to talk about the irregular spelling patterns that the pupils are learning. Noticing the 'quirks' in words will help pupils remember how to spell the words correctly. For example, Gina might point out that ' *"Canoe" looks as if it rhymes with "toe"*', and Harry might add '*So you could say "I dropped the can-oe on my t-oe" and make it rhyme!*'

Similar opportunities for promoting spelling skills by *discussion*, *coaching* and *support* occur throughout this book.

Spelling as a key sub-skill of writing

The development of good spelling may require a considerable investment of time and effort but, once achieved, pays dividends in clear, accurate and confident writing.

Users' guide to *Spotlight on Spelling*

Ethical and inclusive teaching

All the activities in this book have been carefully written to provide teachers with ethical, responsible and inclusive teaching materials. Although the main purpose of each item is to promote the development of your pupils' spelling skills, the materials do, where possible, also promote social responsibility, personal resourcefulness and thoughtfulness towards others.

The use of language related to popular culture (such as superheroes or fantasy), the supernatural, specific religious beliefs or inappropriate role models has been avoided.

Active learning

All activities involve the pupil in active participation in the spelling task. Although some activities require the pupils to copy words, this is only ever in preparation for another activity, such as dictation, where their recall of the spelling pattern will be extended. Incorrect spellings are only used sparingly, and only for the purpose of having the pupils detect the correct spelling from among a set of words. This is because asking pupils to focus on an incorrect spelling (in the absence of the correct version) tends to confuse rather than assist the pupil.

Flexibility

Teachers can draw activities from any section, in any order, according to the needs of a particular group of pupils. For example, a teacher may want to concentrate on exception or irregular words and so may use several of the 'Tough words' (Chapter 4) activities in quick succession. Another teacher may be aware that some of his or her pupils have limited skills in phonological awareness skills and so decide to draw on the activities in 'Listening for sounds' (Chapter 2).

Ease and speed of use

The book is ready for instant teaching. The only preparation required is for the teacher to preselect the appropriate activity for the class, group or individual.

The activities provide a variety of valuable spelling experiences that can form the basis of a single lesson or series of lessons. They are often quick to do and ideally suited to short sessions, where one or more levels of items can be given to the class as a whole, or a selected group of pupils as required. Many activities are also perfect for a quick, intensive burst of spelling when there are only a few minutes to spare.

Teaching notes

The teaching notes at the start of each activity provide teachers with a brief rationale for the activity and practical teaching hints. In some situations suggested correct answers, sample answers or guides are provided for the teacher's convenience.

Emphasis on print not illustrations

Illustrations are not used to support pupils' spelling in this book. Why is that? The reason is simple. In this book we are helping pupils to use printed words. We want to encourage the pupils to focus on the print and to do this we keep illustrations in the background, so that the pupils depend on the print itself.

Worksheets

Teachers are given permission to copy any activity for use with the pupils they teach.

Teachers can identify different levels of difficulty, or different volumes of work. For instance, one pupil might be asked to attempt only Level 1, or the teacher might circle the specific items in an activity that the pupil is required to complete. Alternatively, the teacher may set a given number of items to complete, for example '*Choose any six questions from this sheet.*'

Teachers of pupils with special needs may find it useful to work through the activity with the pupil on one worksheet and then use a clean copy of the worksheet for the pupil to work through the same task again independently.

Making connections

All learning works best if it is connected to other learning. The exchange and cross-fertilisation of emerging skills that occur within a classroom can create a powerful network of interlinked learning.

The activities in this book are specifically directed at spelling, but teachers will find that they can create links with reading, spelling, spoken language and other incidental and formal spelling activities that occur within the classroom. For example, the class may have worked on *Prefixes* (Activity 10), which the teacher can link into one pupil's spelling:

> Look carefully; see the first part of the word? Does that remind you of your spelling? Remember the word 'unzip'? Look, now you have another word that starts with 'un'.

Or in general class discussion the teacher may show how the prefix *un* can be used to create opposites, such as untidy, unreal and undone.

Follow-on activities

The activities are carefully constructed to provide pupils with appropriate spelling activities. Many teachers will find it useful to devise other, similar activities involving current classroom topics, using the activities in this book as a model.

Approximate age levels

Learn your own words (Activity 24) and *Seven in a row* (Activity 25) are independent of spelling level, and can be used to individualise any pupil's spelling programme.

Other activities are presented in levels. There are no hard and fast rules about which particular activities should be given to children of a particular age or spelling level. The activities are flexible and open to teachers to use in a variety of ways with a wide range of ages and abilities. However, the chart below gives a guide to the approximate levels usually appropriate for different spelling ages.

Indication of levels appropriate for given spelling ages			
Spelling age	**Level 1**	**Level 2**	**Level 3**
5.5 to 6.5 years	**Usually quite easy**	**Likely to present some challenges**	**Likely to be very challenging**
	Some teacher support may be needed	Pupils will need some teacher support	Pupils will need a high level of teacher support
6.5 to 8 years	**Easy**	**Usually quite easy**	**Likely to present some challenges**
	Good for consolidation and practice of basic skills Good for explicit teaching of strategies and techniques before moving on to the more difficult levels	Some teacher support may be needed	May work well as extension activity for some pupils Most pupils will need some teacher support
8+ years	**Very easy**	**Usually quite easy**	**Likely to present some challenges**
	Good for pupils who need a high level of explicit teaching and support despite reasonably adequate spelling skills	Good for consolidation and practice of basic skills Good for explicit teaching of strategies and techniques	Some pupils will need teacher support on occasion

CHAPTER 2

Listening for sounds

An essential foundation

Many beginning learners do not readily perceive the individual sounds within words and may, for example, think that a word such as *cat* is just one sound. If the pupil is still at this stage, they must learn to spell every word as a new and unique task. In this situation there is no crossover of learning between *cat* and *bat* because the pupil does not understand the relationship between these two words.

One of the key foundation skills for spelling (and reading) is the ability to recognise and work with the *phonemes* (units of sound) within words. Being able to segment words into their constituent sounds provides a solid starting point for accurate spelling. Individual differences in this skill (called *phonological awareness*) can make all the difference between a pupil succeeding or failing in the early stages of literacy development.

All pupils, especially those with difficulties or special needs, will benefit from explicit, supported practice in making an analysis of the sounds within words and in learning how to manipulate these sounds. This ability to recognise the sounds within a word can then be combined with the skills needed to write the target word down.

Activity 1 provides pupils with explicit practice in listening to words and identifying sounds within words. This promotes good phonological awareness in all pupils, which in turn underpins accurate spelling.

Activities 2–7 further develop the pupils' ability to manipulate sounds in words. This allows learning from one known spelling to generalise to other spellings that share the same phonological pattern. The most basic repeated pattern in spelling is referred to as an *onset and rime* (or *rhyme*), where the onset letter is teamed up with a rime such as *at*, *ay*, *im* or *op*. In this chapter the skills of working with onset and rime are explicitly taught and practised. By Level 3 of each of these activities the challenge extends from simple onset–rime words to introduce more challenging phonemic manipulations by working with multi-syllable words.

The ability to manipulate sounds goes beyond exchanging one initial sound for another. Middle and final sounds can also be manipulated to help the pupil generalise learning from one word to another. *Step* can be changed to *stop*, and *leading* can be changed to *loading*, simply by removing some sounds and replacing them with others. The process of doing this deliberately and being able to describe the process is an important element in teaching pupils to be thoughtful, skilled spellers, who understand how the system works and can use it to their advantage. You can give your pupils explicit teaching and practice in this skill by using the following activities.

Activity 1: Do we need this sound?

Teaching notes

Do we need this sound? is an auditory activity designed to develop the pupils' skills in listening to words and then detecting the sounds contained in those words. This is the beginning point for spelling. In order to complete the items, the pupils will need to be able to segment each word into a sequence of sounds and then compare those sounds with the one given. This is an excellent activity for the development of phonological awareness.

In this activity the teacher and pupils can talk together and discuss each word. The teacher has the opportunity to teach skills in word segmentation, and pupils can also try various sounds to see if they 'fit' the word or not. This is exactly the process they will need to use for spelling.

For example, Joseph may think that *bark* does need a *g* as its final sound. The teacher can help Joseph to break the word into segments and listen carefully to the final sound and hear the subtle difference between *g* and *k*.

Some pupils may find it hard to detect the difference between similar sounds. It is particularly important for the teacher to pronounce the words and the sounds clearly. The sounds are written down for the pupils to refer to, but the teacher must also say each sound because not all pupils will necessarily know the sound values of the written letters. It is a good idea to arrange for a hearing test if you suspect that a pupil has a hearing difficulty. Other pupils may hear well enough, but may have problems with auditory discrimination, and so will need careful teaching and plenty of practice in this area.

Here are the teacher's charts needed for this activity.

Level 1

	Teacher reads this word	Teacher says this sound	
1	wet	c	no
2	sing	s	yes
3	cut	i	no
4	jam	n	no
5	flag	l	yes
6	hand	a	yes
7	bark	g	no
8	twin	w	yes
9	best	u	no

Level 2

	Teacher reads this word	Teacher says this sound	
1	spoon	oo	yes
2	goal	c	no
3	fresh	ch	no
4	sprint	i	yes
5	feast	sh	no
6	storm	er	no
7	crawl	aw	yes
8	smart	d	no
9	toast	oa	yes

Level 3

	Teacher reads this word	Teacher says this sound	
1	leaves	ea	yes
2	porridge	w	no
3	scramble	am	yes
4	smartest	ar	yes
5	roundabout	ou	yes
6	butterfly	it	no
7	ointment	oi	yes
8	express	g	no
9	responsible	is	no

Activity 1

Do we need this sound?

LEVEL 1

	Listen while the teacher reads this word	Listen while the teacher says this sound	Do we need this sound? yes or no?	
1		c	yes	no
2		s	yes	no
3		i	yes	no
4		n	yes	no
5		l	yes	no
6		a	yes	no
7		g	yes	no
8		w	yes	no
9		u	yes	no

Activity 1

Do we need this sound?

LEVEL 2

	Listen while the teacher reads this word	Listen while the teacher says this sound	Do we need this sound? yes or no?	
1		oo	yes	no
2		c	yes	no
3		ch	yes	no
4		i	yes	no
5		sh	yes	no
6		er	yes	no
7		aw	yes	no
8		d	yes	no
9		oa	yes	no

15

Activity 1

Do we need this sound?

LEVEL 3

	Listen while the teacher reads this word	Listen while the teacher says this sound	Do we need this sound? yes or no?	
1		ea	yes	no
2		w	yes	no
3		am	yes	no
4		ar	yes	no
5		ou	yes	no
6		it	yes	no
7		oi	yes	no
8		g	yes	no
9		is	yes	no

Activity 2: Change the first sound

Teaching notes

Change the first sound is a phonological activity that introduces work with onset and rime. The purpose of the activity is to have the pupil look at a printed word on their worksheet and, with the teacher's help (if needed), read that word. The teacher then reads out another word that shares the same rime or ending, but that has a different onset sound or first syllable. The pupil's task is to make a mental analysis of the two words, detect the difference, make the necessary exchange of sounds and write the new word down. This is called *phoneme substitution* and is a very effective teaching tool for developing every pupil's ability to manipulate sounds in words and then follow through by spelling a new word correctly.

The steps in this activity are:

- *Step 1*: Pupil and teacher look at the sample word in the first column and read it aloud.
- *Step 2*: The teacher reads the new word from the second column.
- *Step 3*: The pupil writes down the new word, substituting a new sound for the previous one.

Here are the teacher's charts needed for this activity.

Level 1

	Sample word for pupil to look at	Teacher reads this word to the pupil
1	dog	fog
2	ham	jam
3	back	sack
4	pay	day
5	bell	yell
6	sick	tick
7	bag	flag
8	chip	ship
9	jab	crab

Level 2

	Sample word for pupil to look at	Teacher reads this word to the pupil
1	ring	sing
2	jump	grump
3	crown	drown
4	crust	trust
5	stung	swung
6	punch	crunch
7	slave	wave
8	seed	speed
9	snail	tail

Level 3

	Sample word for pupil to look at	Teacher reads this word to the pupil
1	grudge	smudge
2	health	wealth
3	destruction	construction
4	expecting	rejecting
5	strength	length
6	exported	imported
7	straining	draining
8	glowing	throwing
9	production	introduction

Activity 2

Change the first sound

LEVEL 1

	Look at sample word	<u>Listen</u> and <u>write</u> what you hear	
1	dog	_____	
2	ham	_____	
3	back	_____	
4	pay	_____	
5	bell	_____	
6	sick	_____	
7	bag	_____	
8	chip	_____	
9	jab	_____	

From: *Spotlight on Spelling*, Routledge © Glynis Hannell 2009

Activity 2

Change the first sound

LEVEL 2

Look at the sample word	Listen and write what you hear	
1 ring	_____	
2 jump	_____	
3 crown	_____	
4 crust	_____	
5 stung	_____	
6 punch	_____	
7 slave	_____	
8 seed	_____	
9 snail	_____	

Activity 2

Change the first sound

LEVEL 3

Look at the sample word	Listen and write what you hear	
1 grudge	_____	
2 health	_____	
3 destruction	_____	
4 expecting	_____	
5 strength	_____	
6 exported	_____	
7 straining	_____	
8 glowing	_____	
9 production	_____	

Activity 3: Listen and write real words

Teaching notes

Listen and write real words follows exactly the same method as Activity 2, but this time the pupil is asked to write down four words that use the same rime or final syllable. This expands the skill developed in Activity 2.

The teacher and pupil look at the sample word. Then the teacher reads out the other four words for the pupil to write down.

Here are the teacher's charts needed for this activity.

Level 1

	Sample word for pupil to look at	Teacher reads these words to the pupil			
1	fan	man	pan	can	ran
2	net	jet	bet	wet	pet
3	bill	hill	will	pill	fill
4	hop	top	mop	cop	pop
5	bug	jug	mug	tug	plug
6	hen	pen	men	ten	den
7	map	cap	tap	slap	gap
8	dot	cot	hot	spot	pot
9	kick	pick	lick	stick	tick

Level 2

	Sample word for pupil to look at	Teacher reads these words to the pupil			
1	park	bark	dark	shark	spark
2	lamp	camp	damp	stamp	tramp
3	beach	teach	peach	reach	each
4	beak	weak	creak	freak	speak
5	lift	gift	swift	sift	drift
6	time	lime	slime	crime	chime
7	joke	poke	smoke	woke	broke
8	boat	coat	goat	float	oat
9	bump	jump	plump	stump	dump

Level 3

	Sample word for pupil to look at	Teacher reads these words to the pupil			
1	pain	gain	drain	sprain	explain
2	waste	taste	paste	haste	baste
3	breeze	freeze	sneeze	squeeze	wheeze
4	bench	stench	French	clench	quench
5	witch	pitch	ditch	switch	hitch
6	fringe	twinge	hinge	cringe	binge
7	bought	fought	thought	brought	sought
8	pound	found	hound	ground	sound
9	fudge	nudge	judge	grudge	sludge

Activity 3

Listen and write real words

LEVEL 1

Look at the sample word		Listen and write what you hear			
1	fan				
2	net				
3	bill				
4	hop				
5	bug				
6	hen				
7	map				
8	dot				
9	kick				

From: *Spotlight on Spelling*, Routledge © Glynis Hannell 2009

Activity 3

Listen and write real words

LEVEL 2

Look at the sample word		Listen and write what you hear			
1	park				
2	lamp				
3	beach				
4	beak				
5	lift				
6	time				
7	joke				
8	boat				
9	bump				

Activity 3

Listen and write real words

LEVEL 3

Look at the sample word	Listen and write what you hear			
1 pain				
2 waste				
3 breeze				
4 bench				
5 witch				
6 fringe				
7 bought				
8 pound				
9 fudge				

From: *Spotlight on Spelling*, Routledge © Glynis Hannell 2009

Activity 4: Listen and write nonsense words

Teaching notes

Listen and write nonsense words repeats the same working method as Activities 1 and 2. However, the pupils are now given an even bigger challenge. Instead of writing familiar words, they are asked to write nonsense words. This really makes the pupil think very carefully about the sounds and gives explicit practice in phoneme substitution without the assistance of external prompts.

Here are the teacher's charts needed for this activity.

Level 1

Sample word for pupil to look at	Teacher reads these words to the pupil			
1 dab	bab	hab	gab	mab
2 jam	wam	tam	flam	gam
3 leg	neg	heg	feg	zeg
4 hen	nen	sen	ren	pren
5 pick	bick	fick	zick	plick
6 lid	gid	nid	tid	crid
7 job	wob	tob	pob	stob
8 dog	mog	sog	gog	plog
9 pup	dup	nup	bup	trup

Level 2

Sample word for pupil to look at	Teacher reads these words to the pupil			
1 page	dage	hage	prage	vage
2 face	nace	tace	clace	wace
3 real	leal	treal	jeal	queal
4 help	belp	felp	trelp	velp
5 pink	tink	nink	grink	flink
6 wish	gish	stish	tish	pish
7 corn	norn	storn	jorn	chorn
8 coin	boin	ploin	toin	froin
9 sung	nung	trung	jung	drung

Level 3

Sample word for pupil to look at	Teacher reads these words to the pupil			
1 dawn	blawn	stawn	grawn	clawn
2 meal	treal	gleal	screal	sneal
3 weave	beave	skeave	teave	screave
4 hedge	bedge	stredge	pedge	tredge
5 nine	hine	trine	jine	prine
6 wish	bish	nish	crish	flish
7 robe	stobe	wobe	chobe	trobe
8 coach	boach	noach	stroach	toach
9 sung	nung	chung	plung	trung

Activity 4

Listen and write nonsense words

LEVEL 1

Look at the sample word	Listen and write what you hear			
1 dab				
2 jam				
3 leg				
4 hen				
5 pick				
6 lid				
7 job				
8 dog				
9 pup				

From: *Spotlight on Spelling*, Routledge © Glynis Hannell 2009

Activity 4

Listen and write nonsense words

LEVEL 2

Look at the sample word	Listen and write what you hear			
1 page				
2 face				
3 real				
4 help				
5 pink				
6 wish				
7 corn				
8 coin				
9 sung				

Activity 4

Listen and write nonsense words

LEVEL 3

Look at the sample word	**Listen and write what you hear**			
1 dawn				
2 meal				
3 weave				
4 hedge				
5 nine				
6 wish				
7 robe				
8 coach				
9 sung				

From: *Spotlight on Spelling*, Routledge © Glynis Hannell 2009

Activity 5: Change the middle sound

Teaching notes

In *Change the middle sound* the pupils are asked once again to exchange one sound for another, but this time they are working with middle sounds. Many pupils find middle sounds particularly difficult to handle. Often the middle sound is a soft, vowel sound and the variations between one sound and another, for example between *a* and *u*, can be very subtle. Talking with the pupils and helping them to listen very carefully will develop good skills that will underpin good spelling.

Discussing *how* the word is transformed is a very useful teaching technique. For example, a pupil may explain '*You have to take out the "oa" sound and put in "oo" to change "boat" to "boot".*' This helps to make the process explicit and helps all pupils to understand how to use one word to create another.

Here are the teacher's charts needed for this activity.

Level 1			*Level 2*			*Level 3*	
Sample word for pupil to look at	**Teacher reads this word to the pupil**		**Sample word for pupil to look at**	**Teacher reads this word to the pupil**		**Sample word for pupil to look at**	**Teacher reads this word to the pupil**
1 cup	cap		1 chick	chuck		1 master	mister
2 bat	bit		2 boat	boot		2 hurdle	handle
3 pen	pin		3 lace	lice		3 squashed	squirmed
4 dig	dog		4 grain	groan		4 leading	loading
5 top	tap		5 small	smell		5 quality	qualify
6 mad	mud		6 torn	turn		6 knitting	knotting
7 sack	sick		7 lump	limp		7 dismay	display
8 step	stop		8 foot	feet		8 power	powder
9 chip	chop		9 shout	shoot		9 correction	connection

Activity 5

Change the middle sound

LEVEL 1

Look at the sample word	Listen and write what you hear	
1 cup	_____	
2 bat	_____	
3 pen	_____	
4 dig	_____	
5 top	_____	
6 mad	_____	
7 sack	_____	
8 step	_____	
9 chip	_____	

From: *Spotlight on Spelling*, Routledge © Glynis Hannell 2009

Activity 5

Change the middle sound

LEVEL 2

Look at the sample word	**Listen and write what you hear**	
1 chick	_____	
2 boat	_____	
3 lace	_____	
4 grain	_____	
5 small	_____	
6 torn	_____	
7 lump	_____	
8 foot	_____	
9 shout	_____	

Activity 5

Change the middle sound

LEVEL 3

Look at the sample word	<u>Listen</u> and <u>write</u> what you hear	
1 master	_____	
2 hurdle	_____	
3 squashed	_____	
4 leading	_____	
5 quality	_____	
6 knitting	_____	
7 dismay	_____	
8 power	_____	
9 correction	_____	

From: *Spotlight on Spelling*, Routledge © Glynis Hannell 2009

Activity 6: Change the last sound

Teaching notes

Change the last sound is another activity for practising phonemic exchange. This time the pupils focus on the final sounds of the words, and exchange one final sound for another. As with all these activities, the pupil needs to make a good phonological analysis of the sounds in the words to be able to identify the old sound and then new sound to make the exchange.

Here are the teacher's charts needed for this activity.

Level 1

	Sample word for pupil to look at	Teacher reads this word to the pupil
1	dog	dot
2	rat	ran
3	spin	spit
4	mud	mum
5	wish	win
6	jack	jam
7	help	held
8	play	plan
9	kick	kid

Level 2

	Sample word for pupil to look at	Teacher reads this word to the pupil
1	chair	chain
2	crop	cross
3	green	greed
4	sweet	sweep
5	date	dame
6	place	plane
7	wish	witch
8	squeal	squeak
9	crust	crush

Level 3

	Sample word for pupil to look at	Teacher reads this word to the pupil
1	pump	punt
2	dunce	dutch
3	journey	journal
4	gentleman	gentleness
5	mistake	mischief
6	educated	education
7	complete	complain
8	telegram	telegraph
9	electricity	electrician

Activity 6

Change the last sound

LEVEL 1

Look at the sample word	**Listen and write what you hear**	
1 dog	_____	
2 rat	_____	
3 spin	_____	
4 mud	_____	
5 wish	_____	
6 jack	_____	
7 help	_____	
8 play	_____	
9 kick	_____	

From: *Spotlight on Spelling*, Routledge © Glynis Hannell 2009

Activity 6

Change the last sound

LEVEL 2

Look at the sample word	Listen and write what you hear	
1 chair	_____	
2 crop	_____	
3 green	_____	
4 sweet	_____	
5 date	_____	
6 place	_____	
7 wish	_____	
8 squeal	_____	
9 crust	_____	

Activity 6

Change the last sound

LEVEL 3

Look at the sample word	**<u>Listen</u> and <u>write</u> what you hear**	
1 pump	_____	
2 dunce	_____	
3 journey	_____	
4 gentleman	_____	
5 mistake	_____	
6 educated	_____	
7 complete	_____	
8 telegram	_____	
9 electricity	_____	

From: *Spotlight on Spelling*, Routledge © Glynis Hannell 2009

CHAPTER 3

Letters and sounds

Building blocks for spelling

Chapter 2 introduced activities to promote your pupils' phonological awareness. In Chapter 3 the emphasis is on developing your pupils' ability to use printed letters to represent the phonological patterns in words. Although not all words in English have a regular spelling pattern, many do. Pupils who understand how to work with sounds (and the letters that represent the sounds) will be stronger spellers than pupils who rely on rote learning and a 'whole word' approach.

However, there will be wide individual differences in your pupils' ability to learn the necessary skills. To some, very fortunate, pupils the relationship between speech sounds and spelling patterns will come very easily. However, for many pupils this is an area of literacy that needs particular care. Explicit links between speech sounds and spelling, plenty of discussion and strong scaffolding for learning, combined with many opportunities for practice, will all be important. Making the spelling activities relevant to the pupils' own experiences and interests will also help. For example, the teacher may be able to relate spelling patterns in this chapter to pupils' names or interests,

thus: '*Look "Harry" has a "y", just like the words in this list*'; or '*See if you can find anything in your lunch box that has an "ee" or an "ea" sound in it.*'

Sounds at the end of a word are often strong and relatively easy for pupils to 'hear' and so word endings form the basis of *Word endings* (Activity 7), which is the first, introductory activity in this chapter on 'Letters and sounds'. This is followed by *Long sounds (1)* and *(2)* (Activities 8 and 9), which work with the much more difficult long vowel sounds. These sounds are often very subtle and hard to discriminate and they can often be written in various ways. For example, compare the sounds in *beat*, *boat* and *bait*; in each word the long vowel sound *ea*, *oa* or *ai* is 'soft' (or *unvoiced*) and each contains the letter *a* when written down.

Prefixes, Rules for suffixes, Plurals and *Compound words* (Activities 10–13) focus on the use of *morphemes*. Morphemes are the smallest units of speech that have meaning. Research has shown that pupils taught to use morphemes and apply the rules for their use in spelling develop better skills than pupils who have not been taught to do so. Prefixes, suffixes and compound words are introduced at this stage.

Activity 7: Word endings

Teaching notes

Word endings is designed to provide pupils with an opportunity to work with families of words that share common word endings, in this case distinctive vowel + consonant sounds. The steps in this activity are:

• *Step 1: Sound out the letter clusters*
With the teacher's support the pupils look at the letter clusters in the second column of the chart. Teachers can use this stage of the activity to teach or remind the pupils of the sound associated with each cluster of letters, for example '*That's right! Those letters make the "ell" sound, so you are looking for words with "ell" in them.*'

• *Step 2: Find the letter clusters in the words*
Pupils look for groups of letters, such as *ack*, *ain* or *udge* in each sentence. The pupils are asked to circle or highlight each target letter cluster that they find within the sentence.

• *Step 3: Read the sentences aloud*
The next stage is for the teacher and pupils to read the sentence aloud to make sure that everyone understands the words that they are about to copy. Good teaching points will arise in doing this; for example, some pupils will need help with word decoding skills, vocabulary development and so on: '*Say those sounds over again and push them together: st-i-ck; that's it, st-ick, stick*'; or '*Does anyone know what the word "freight" means?*'; or '*What is a bangle . . . what does jangle mean?*'; and so on.

Before any pupil attempts to copy the sentences the teacher should be confident that they can read all the words. This ensures that the exercise is meaningful, even though some of the sentences are often silly, for example *The bug and the slug gave each other a hug.* Word families are embedded in sentences to help pupils to remember the sets of words that belong together, for example *chick*, *trick*, *brick* and *stick*. This helps to build spelling skills.

• *Step 4: Copy each sentence*
Once the pupils have circled the letter clusters in each word and read the sentences, they are asked to copy each sentence out for themselves. A blank line is left in the chart for the pupils to copy the sentence. This process helps to consolidate the skills in using the same letter cluster for a series of words sharing the same pattern.

• *Step 5 (optional): Follow-up activities*
Many pupils will benefit from additional work. The teacher can vary the amount and type of follow-up work to meet individual needs. Some pupils may benefit from extra time spent talking to the teacher about the sounds in the words, while others may need extra practice at writing the words down. Teachers can use the words from this activity in follow-up spelling work, such as dictation of the word sets (without the originals to copy), spelling lists to learn, sentence writing to include the spelling words, anagrams and so on.

The teacher's charts needed for this activity are shown on the facing page.

Level 1

1	ay	You can stay and play all day. Hurray!
2	ox	There is a fox in a box with chickenpox.
3	ell	Yell! Yell. Ring the bell. Nell has fallen in the well.
4	ack	Stack your backpack on the rack.
5	ick	The chick has a trick with a brick and a stick.
6	ing	The king's ring is on a string.
7	uck	The duck is stuck in the truck in the muck.
8	ug	The bug and the slug gave each other a hug.
9	in	Spin the pin in the bin.

Level 2

1	amp	The tramp hid a lamp in his camp by the ramp.
2	ast	Ben ran past very fast but he was still last.
3	ane	Jane used a crane to get into the plane.
4	ake	It's a mistake to bake a cake for a snake.
5	ain	The rain in Spain falls mainly down the drain.
6	ide	The wide bride had a ride on the slide
7	ink	I think this pink drink stinks of ink.
8	oose	The goose and the moose were out on the loose.
9	unch	Make a crunch, crunch, crunch when you munch your lunch.

Level 3

1	udge	There's a smudge on this fudge that just will not budge.
2	angle	Bangles that jangle will get in a tangle.
3	ound	The hound cleared the mound with one mighty bound.
4	ight	The knight got a fright when his tights caught alight.
5	umble	Don't grumble if you stumble or tumble in the dark.
6	iggle	Do you giggle, wiggle or wriggle when you dance?
7	eight	The weight of this freight is over eight tonnes.
8	tion	Did I mention a potion or a lotion will cure the affliction.
9	ect	I expect the insect will detect the trap.

Activity 7

Word endings

LEVEL 1

<u>Listen</u> carefully to your teacher, who will tell you what to do.

1 ay   You can stay and play all day. Hurray!

_____

2 ox   There is a fox in a box with chickenpox.

_____

3 ell   Yell! Yell. Ring the bell. Nell has fallen in the well.

_____

4 ack   Stack your backpack on the rack.

_____

5 ick   The chick has a trick with a brick and a stick.

_____

6 ing   The king's ring is on a string.

_____

7 uck   The duck is stuck in the truck in the muck.

_____

8 ug   The bug and the slug gave each other a hug.

_____

9 in   Spin the pin in the bin.

_____

From: *Spotlight on Spelling*, Routledge © Glynis Hannell 2009

Activity 7

Word endings

Listen carefully to your teacher, who will tell you what to do.

LEVEL 2

1 amp The tramp hid a lamp in his camp by the ramp.

_____

2 ast Ben ran past very fast but he was still last.

_____

3 ane Jane used a crane to get into the plane.

_____

4 ake It's a mistake to bake a cake for a snake.

_____

5 ain The rain in Spain falls mainly down the drain.

_____

6 ide The wide bride had a ride on the slide.

_____

7 ink I think this pink drink stinks of ink.

_____

8 oose The goose and the moose were out on the loose.

_____

9 unch Make a crunch, crunch, crunch when you munch your lunch.

_____

Activity 7

Word endings

Listen carefully to your teacher, who will tell you
what to do.

LEVEL 3

1   udge   There's a smudge on this fudge that just will not budge.

_____

2   angle   Bangles that jangle will get in a tangle.

_____

3   ound   The hound cleared the mound with one mighty bound.

_____

4   ight   The knight got a fright when his tights caught alight.

_____

5   umble Don't grumble if you stumble or tumble in the dark.

_____

6   iggle   Do you giggle, wiggle or wriggle when you dance?

_____

7   eight   The weight of this freight is over eight tonnes.

_____

8   tion   Did I mention a potion or a lotion will cure the
affliction?

_____

9   ect   I expect the insect will detect the trap.

_____

   From: _Spotlight on Spelling_, Routledge © Glynis Hannell 2009

Activity 8: Long sounds (1)

Teaching notes

Long sounds (1) is designed to provide pupils with an opportunity to work with families of words that contain a range of long vowel sounds. The steps in this activity are:

- *Step 1: Sound out the letter clusters*
With the teacher's support the pupils look at the letter clusters in the second column of the chart. Teachers can use this stage of the activity to teach or remind the pupils of the sound associated with each cluster of letters, for example '*That's right! Those letters make the "ee" sound, so all the words on this line have the "ee" sound.*'

- *Step 2: Find the letter clusters in the words*
Pupils look for groups of letters, such as *ee*, *ie* or *ure* in each word. The pupils are asked to circle or highlight each letter cluster that they find within each word. Particular care is needed in teaching the *silent e* words. The sound is shown as *a_e*, *i_e* or *e_e*. Marking the three-letter cluster (which includes the two letters given plus one other letter, e.g. *ake*, *ise*, *ene*) will help pupils to recognise this particular spelling pattern in words.

Items 6 and 7 in Level 3 will need teachers to work with the pupils to discuss how the same letter *y* can have either the long *e* sound (as in *cherry*) or the long *i* sound as in *apply*.

- *Step 3: Read the words aloud*
The next stage is for the pupils to read the words aloud to make sure they understand the words that they are about to copy.

Teachers can use this as an opportunity to promote word decoding skills and word knowledge.

Before any pupil attempts to copy the words the teacher should be confident that they can read all the words. This ensures that the exercise makes sense to every pupil.

- *Step 4: Copy each set of words*
Once the pupils have circled the letter clusters in each word, they are asked to copy each set of words out for themselves. A blank line is left in the chart for the pupils to do this. This process helps to consolidate the skills in using the same letter cluster for a series of words sharing the same pattern.

- *Step 5 (optional): Follow-up activities*
Some pupils will only need the activities described above to master the principles being taught. However, many pupils will benefit from additional work. The teacher can vary the amount and type of follow-up work to meet individual needs. Some pupils may benefit from extra time spent talking to the teacher about the sounds in the words, while others may need extra practice at writing the words down. Teachers can use the words from this activity in follow-up spelling work, such as dictation of the word sets (without the originals to copy), spelling lists to learn, sentence writing to include the spelling words, anagrams and so on.

The teacher's charts needed for this activity are shown on the next page.

Level 1

1	ay	day, may, say, hay, play, stay, way
2	ai	nail, mail, tail, wait, main
3	a_e	game, cave, hate, tame, wave, date, late
4	a_e	lake, name, take, safe, cane, same, tape
5	ee	bee, see, keep, peel, keep, week, peek
6	ea	pea, sea, tea, beak, heat, leaf, real
7	ie	pie, tie, lie, die
8	y	my, by, sky, fly, try, cry, dry, spy
9	i_e	bike, ride, dive, like, mice, five, pipe

Level 2

1	ai	brain, explain, email, claim, trailer, plain, grain
2	a_e	pancake, escape, cabbage, palace, pirate, voyage
3	ee	beekeeper, agree, squeeze, screech, seaweed
4	ea	dream, easy, wheat, speak, greasy, breathe, steamed
5	e_e	scene, these, delete, swede, scheme, obese
6	ie	piece, believe, babies, bodies, movie, pixie, cities
7	y	funny, grumpy, dizzy, jelly, lucky, silly, easy, cherry
8	igh	sigh, flight, night, bright, night, tight, light, might
9	i_e	invite, excite, bonfire, realise, stripe, collide, divide

Level 3

1	a	cola, boa, spa, yoga, puma, tuba, era, soda, data
2	eigh	weigh, neigh, sleigh
3	ey	they, obey, fey, grey, prey, whey, hey
4	ee	absentee, succeeded, goalkeeper, cartwheel, sixteenth
5	ie	niece, siege, grief, shield, priest, chief
6	y	cherry, cloudy, canary, family, artery, bakery, beauty, canopy
7	y	satisfy, occupy, multiply, apply, magnify, terrify, horrify
8	ure	nature, future, measure, treasure, lecture, texture
9	ui	penguin, anguish, extinguish, vanquish, linguist

Activity 8

Long sounds (1)

Listen carefully to your teacher, who will tell you what to do.

LEVEL 1

1 ay   day, may, say, hay, play, stay, way

_____

2 ai   nail, mail, tail, wait, main

_____

3 a_e   game, cave, hate, tame, wave, date, late

_____

4 a_e   lake, name, take, safe, cane, same, tape

_____

5 ee   bee, see, keep, peel, keep, week, peek

_____

6 ea   pea, sea, tea, beak, heat, leaf, real

_____

7 ie   pie, tie, lie, die

_____

8 y   my, by, sky, fly, try, cry, dry, spy

_____

9 i_e   bike, ride, dive, like, mice, five, pipe

_____

Activity 8

Long sounds (1)

<u>Listen</u> carefully to your teacher, who will tell you
what to do.

1 ai brain, explain, email, claim, trailer, plain, grain

_____

2 a_e pancake, escape, cabbage, palace, pirate, voyage

_____

3 ee beekeeper, agree, squeeze, screech, seaweed

_____

4 ea dream, easy, wheat, speak, greasy, breathe, steamed

_____

5 e_e scene, these, delete, swede, scheme, obese

_____

6 ie piece, believe, babies, bodies, movie, pixie, cities

_____

7 y funny, grumpy, dizzy, jelly, lucky, silly, easy, cherry

_____

8 igh sigh, flight, night, bright, night, tight, light, might

_____

9 i_e invite, excite, bonfire, realise, stripe, collide, divide

_____

Activity 8

Long sounds (1)

Listen carefully to your teacher, who will tell you
what to do.

1 a cola, boa, spa, yoga, puma, tuba, era, soda, data

_____

2 eigh weigh, neigh, sleigh

_____

3 ey they, obey, fey, grey, prey, whey, hey

_____

4 ee absentee, succeeded, goalkeeper, cartwheel, sixteenth

_____

5 ie niece, siege, grief, shield, priest, chief

_____

6 y cherry, cloudy, canary, family, artery, bakery, beauty,
canopy

_____

7 y satisfy, occupy, multiply, apply, magnify, terrify, horrify

_____

8 ure nature, future, measure, treasure, lecture, texture

_____

9 ui penguin, anguish, extinguish, vanquish, linguist

_____

Activity 9: Long sounds (2)

Teaching notes

Long sounds (2) is designed to provide pupils with a further opportunity to work with families of words that contain a range of long vowel sounds. The steps in this activity are:

• *Step 1: Sound out the letter clusters*
With the teacher's support the pupils look at the letter clusters in the second column of the chart. Teachers can use this stage of the activity to teach or remind the pupils of the sound associated with each cluster of letters: *'That's right! Those letters make the "ew" sound, so all the words on this line have the "ew" sound.'*

• *Step 2: Find the letter clusters in the words*
Pupils look for groups of letters, such as *o_e*, *aw* or *ui* in each word. The pupils are asked to circle or highlight each letter cluster that they find within each word. Particular care is needed for the *silent e* words. The sound is shown as *o_e*. Marking the three-letter cluster (which includes the two letters given plus one other letter, e.g. *ole*, *ome*, *oke*) will help pupils to recognise this particular spelling pattern in words.

Items 5 and 6 in Level 1 provide teachers with the opportunity to talk to pupils about how the same letters can sometimes have two (or more) sound values. It is useful for pupils to see that there are two groups of words that share the same pattern, but that have slightly different ways of being pronounced. Some pronunciation variations will be regional in the UK; for example, the word *book* can have either the short or the long *oo* sound depending on which regional accent is used.

• *Step 3: Read the words aloud*
The next stage is for the pupils to read the words aloud to make sure that they understand the words they are about to copy. Teachers can use this as an opportunity to promote word-decoding skills and word knowledge.

Before any pupil attempts to copy the words, the teacher should be confident that they can read all the words. This ensures that the exercise makes sense to every pupil.

• *Step 4: Copy each set of words*
Once the pupils have circled the letter clusters in each word, they are asked to copy each set of words out for themselves. A blank line is left in the chart for the pupils to do this. This process helps to consolidate the skills in using the same letter cluster for a series of words sharing the same pattern.

• *Step 5 (optional): Follow-up activities*
Many pupils will benefit from additional work. The teacher can vary the amount and type of follow-up work to meet individual needs. Some pupils may benefit from extra time spent talking to the teacher about the sounds in the words, while others may need extra practice at writing the words down. Teachers can use the words from this activity in follow-up spelling work, such as dictation of the word sets (without the originals to copy), spelling lists to learn, sentence writing to include the spelling words, anagrams and so on.

The teacher's charts needed for this activity are shown on the facing page.

Level 1

1	oy	boy, toy, soy, joy
2	oa	boat, coat, loaf, road, soap, toad
3	o_e	joke, nose, pole, zone, home, hole, mole
4	ow	cow, now, how, bow
5	oo	zoo, too, pool, soon, boot, root, moon, loop
6	oo	good, wood, book, wool, foot, took, hook
7	ew	few, new, flew, blew
8	ar	car, bar, tar, far, jar, star
9	aw	paw, law, saw, jaw, raw, seesaw

Level 2

1	oi	oil, soil, spoil, foil, coin, join, avoid
2	oa	throat, toast, coach, poach, roast, groan
3	o_e	stone, remote, throne, tadpole, primrose, jawbone
4	oo	choose, goose, tooth, spoon, choose, smooth
5	oo	poor, door, moor, floor
6	ow	mow, tow, row, low, crow, flow, grow, slow, show
7	ew	threw, knew, drew, chew, screw, view
8	ue	blue, clue, due, glue, true
9	aw	jigsaw, straw, macaw, pawpaw, rickshaw, jackdaw

Level 3

1	oi	ointment, disappointment, checkpoint, exploit, rejoice
2	oa	cockroach, overload, slowcoach, crossroad, afloat
3	o_e	beanpole, earphones, diagnose, glucose, bulldoze
4	au	launch, taunt, gaunt, flaunt, haunt, staunch, paunch
5	air	dairy, prairie, stairway, fairy, armchair, despair, funfair
6	ue	statue, avenue, value, rescue, tissue, continue, pursue, queue
7	aw	frogspawn, withdrawn, tomahawk, awesome, awful, awkward
8	ui	fruit, swimsuit, bruise, cruise, recruit, pursuit, sluice
9	or	scorch, explore, anchor, mirror, normal, uniform, decorate

Activity 9

Long sounds (2)

LEVEL 1

<u>Listen</u> carefully to your teacher, who will tell you what to do.

1 oy   boy, toy, soy, joy

_____

2 oa   boat, coat, loaf, road, soap, toad

_____

3 o_e   joke, nose, pole, zone, home, hole, mole

_____

4 ow   cow, now, how, bow

_____

5 oo   zoo, too, pool, soon, boot, root, moon, loop

_____

6 oo   good, wood, book, wool, foot, took, hook

_____

7 ew   few, new, flew, blew

_____

8 ar   car, bar, tar, far, jar, star

_____

9 aw   paw, law, saw, jaw, raw, seesaw

_____

From: *Spotlight on Spelling*, Routledge © Glynis Hannell 2009

Activity 9

Long sounds (2)

Listen carefully to your teacher, who will tell you
what to do.

LEVEL 2

1 oi   oil, soil, spoil, foil, coin, join, avoid

_____

2 oa   throat, toast, coach, poach, roast, groan

_____

3 o_e   stone, remote, throne, tadpole, primrose, jawbone

_____

4 oo   choose, goose, tooth, spoon, choose, smooth

_____

5 oo   poor, door, moor, floor

_____

6 ow   mow, tow, row, low, crow, flow, grow, slow, show

_____

7 ew   threw, knew, drew, chew, screw, view

_____

8 ue   blue, clue, due, glue, true

_____

9 aw   jigsaw, straw, macaw, pawpaw, rickshaw, jackdaw

_____

Activity 9

Long sounds (2)

Listen carefully to your teacher, who will tell you
what to do.

LEVEL 3

1 oi   ointment, disappointment, checkpoint, exploit, rejoice

_____

2 oa   cockroach, overload, slowcoach, crossroad, afloat

_____

3 o_e   beanpole, earphones, diagnose, glucose, bulldoze

_____

4 au   launch, taunt, gaunt, flaunt, haunt, staunch, paunch

_____

5 air   dairy, prairie, stairway, fairy, armchair, despair, funfair

_____

6 ue   statue, avenue, value, rescue, tissue, continue, pursue,
queue

_____

7 aw   frogspawn, withdrawn, tomahawk, awesome, awful,
awkward

_____

8 ui   fruit, swimsuit, bruise, cruise, recruit, pursuit, sluice

_____

9 or   scorch, explore, anchor, mirror, normal, uniform, decorate

_____

From: _Spotlight on Spelling_, Routledge © Glynis Hannell 2009

Activity 10: Prefixes

Teaching notes

Prefixes are *morphemes*, that is they are small groups of letters that have meaning, such as *sub* (*below*), *pre* (*before*) and *anti* (*against*). Prefixes are used to modify a word or alter its meaning.

Understanding how prefixes work helps the pupil to become independent in spelling (and understanding) words that are made up of a base word plus a prefix. For many pupils explicit teaching is needed to establish an awareness of the way compound words, using a prefix, are structured.

The spelling rules for the use of prefixes are, thankfully, uncomplicated. The only exception to this is the prefix *all*, which is modified into *al* in words such as *altogether*, *although* and *alright*. This is not taught in this activity, but can easily be introduced into a spelling lesson on prefixes, asking the pupils to spot the change that occurs to the prefix *all* in these words.

The steps in this activity are:

• *Step 1: 'Unpacking' words*
The pupils and teacher look at the words on the chart. The pupils are asked to 'unpack' each word into a prefix and a base word. The prefixes used are printed above the chart to provide the pupils with scaffolding for the task. Some pupils may need teacher support and guidance, while others may be able to work unaided.

• *Step 2: Filling in the missing words*
The teacher can decide which approach is appropriate for each pupil:

– *Dictation*
This is the best approach for pupils who experience difficulties with reading and written language. For these pupils the teacher reads out each sentence and asks the pupils to fill in the missing word. The pupils can refer back to their work on the chart at the top of their page to check the spelling of the word.

– *Independent work*
This is the best approach for pupils who can cope with the reading requirements of this task easily. They are asked to work on their own, filling in the missing words as appropriate.

• *Step 3 (optional): Follow-up work*
Teachers can use the prefixes and words in this activity for further work. Many pupils will benefit from follow-up, revision work on the words that have been taught. For example, they might have these same words in other spelling activities, they might find other words that use the same prefixes, or they might take part in word-building games in which prefix and base-word cards are assembled to make words.

The teacher's charts needed for this activity are shown on the following page.

Level 1

	Word	Prefix	Base word
1	unzip	un	zip
2	replay	re	play
3	unpack	un	pack
4	redid	re	did
5	unhappy	un	happy
6	subway	sub	way
7	preschool	pre	school
8	inside	in	side
9	untie	un	tie

Dictation (teacher's version)

1 Take off your boots; **untie** the laces first.

2 I will **replay** that song.

3 Help me to **unpack** the shopping.

4 The **subway** is under the ground.

5 It is so hot; **unzip** your coat.

6 Little kids go to **preschool**.

7 Stay **inside** when it is cold.

8 The dog feels **unhappy** because he had to stay at home.

9 I did not like the pattern so I **redid** it.

Level 2

	Word	Prefix	Base word
1	outside	out	side
2	untidy	un	tidy
3	dislike	dis	like
4	television	tele	vision
5	defrost	de	frost
6	misprint	mis	print
7	return	re	turn
8	overcoat	over	coat
9	enjoy	en	joy

Dictation (teacher's version)

1 When do you think that the birds will **return**?

2 I **dislike** the smell of that soap.

3 Put the **television** on in time for the cartoons.

4 I **enjoy** watching you play football.

5 Dad left his **overcoat** on the train.

6 Put the cat **outside** before you go to bed.

7 I must **defrost** the meat before I cook it.

8 There was a **misprint** in the list of names.

9 Your room is so **untidy**.

Level 3

	Word	Prefix	Base word
1	underage	under	age
2	exchange	ex	change
3	forecast	fore	cast
4	submarine	sub	marine
5	antiseptic	anti	septic
6	supersonic	super	sonic
7	hyperactive	hyper	active
8	endanger	en	danger
9	international	inter	national

Dictation (teacher's version)

1 The weather **forecast** said it would rain later.

2 Put some **antiseptic** on your cut before you bandage it.

3 The aircraft was **supersonic**.

4 You will **endanger** other people if you light a fire there.

5 You are not allowed into the cinema if you are **underage**.

6 If you do not like it you can **exchange** it for another.

7 The Olympics is an **international** sports event.

8 The children were **hyperactive** after they had seen the show.

9 The **submarine** travelled under the ice.

Activity 10

Prefixes

Look for the prefixes:
un, **in**, **pre**, **re**, **sub**

LEVEL 1

	Word	Prefix	Base word
1	**unzip**		
2	**replay**		
3	**unpack**		
4	**redid**		
5	**unhappy**		
6	**subway**		
7	**preschool**		
8	**inside**		
9	**untie**		

Fill in the missing words.

1 Take off your boots; _____ the laces first.

2 I will _____ that song.

3 Help me to _____ the shopping.

4 The _____ is under the ground.

5 It is so hot; _____ your coat.

6 Little kids go to _____.

7 Stay _____ when it is cold.

8 The dog feels _____ because he had to stay at home.

9 I did not like the pattern so I _____ it.

Activity 10

Prefixes

<u>Look</u> for the prefixes:

un, **dis**, **mis**, **re**, **en**, **out**, **tele**, **de**, **over**

LEVEL 2

	Word	Prefix	Base word
1	**outside**		
2	**untidy**		
3	**dislike**		
4	**television**		
5	**defrost**		
6	**misprint**		
7	**return**		
8	**overcoat**		
9	**enjoy**		

<u>Fill in</u> the missing words.

1 When do you think that the birds will _____?

2 I _____ the smell of that soap.

3 Put the _____ on in time for the cartoons.

4 I _____ watching you play football.

5 Dad left his _____ on the train.

6 Put the cat _____ before you go to bed.

7 I must _____ the meat before I cook it.

8 There was a _____ in the list of names.

9 Your room is so _____.

Activity 10

Prefixes

Look for the prefixes:

en, **inter**, **ex**, **super**, **hyper**, **under**, **fore**, **sub**, **anti**

LEVEL 3

	Word	Prefix	Base word
1	**underage**		
2	**exchange**		
3	**forecast**		
4	**submarine**		
5	**antiseptic**		
6	**supersonic**		
7	**hyperactive**		
8	**endanger**		
9	**international**		

Fill in the missing words.

1   The weather _____ said it would rain later.

2   Put some _____ on your cut before you bandage it.

3   The aircraft was _____.

4   You will _____ other people if you light a fire there.

5   You are not allowed into the cinema if you are _____.

6   If you do not like it you can _____ it for another.

7   The Olympics is an _____ sports event.

8   The children were _____ after they had seen the show.

9   The _____ travelled under the ice.

Activity 11: Rules for suffixes

Teaching notes

While prefixes are quite straightforward and do not challenge the pupil to remember complex rules, suffixes are quite different. Some suffix rules depend on the structure of the base word. For example, the final consonant of a short word is usually doubled if the word ends in a vowel + consonant combination such as *cut/cutting*. But if the word ends in two consonants then there is no need to double any letters, for example *nest/nesting*. Other rules apply according to the structure of the suffix. For example, words that end with a *silent e* keep their *e* if the suffix starts with a consonant, for example *love/lovely*, but drop their *e* if the suffix begins with a vowel as in *love/loving*.

Complicated isn't it? For pupils who experience learning difficulties or become anxious with unfamiliar tasks, learning or following spelling rules can prove to be quite daunting. And yet, once in possession of these rules, these same pupils will be empowered by their ability to spell words correctly by using the rules they have been taught. The secret is to teach the rules explicitly, with plenty of support, scaffolding and practice.

One important prerequisite is that pupils can work with vowels and consonants. To make this aspect of the task easier, each level of *Rules for suffixes* is given a chart of both for the pupils to refer to.

The spelling rules being practised are clearly given for each level. However, it is not anticipated that teachers will expect pupils to complete these tasks unaided. Many pupils will need a high level of teacher input and guidance to understand and apply the rules. For example, the teacher might first talk to the pupils about the activity, ensuring that words such as *suffix*, *consonant* and *vowel* are understood. After that the teacher will, in all probability, guide the pupils to use the hints given and then give prompts and help where needed.

Level 3 of this activity is challenging. In particular, items 8 and 9 are very difficult. Exceptions to rules are conceptually the most difficult type of rule learning, so teachers might like to reserve these two items for the very advanced pupils or use them as a class activity with a high level of teacher guidance.

There are several other spelling rules governing the use of suffixes, for which there was not enough room in this book. However, teachers can use this activity as a starting point before introducing other rules at a later stage.

Teacher charts are not required for this activity.

Activity 11

Rules for suffixes

LEVEL 1

Consonants						
b	c	d	f	g	h	j
k	l	m	n	p	q	r
s	t	v	w	x	y	z

Vowels				
a	e	i	o	u

Rules for adding suffixes to short words that end in a consonant:

- <u>1 consonant</u> at the end of the word, <u>double the consonant</u>
- <u>2 consonants</u> at the end of the word, <u>don't double the consonant</u>

	Word	Suffix	Write the new word
1	**hit**	**ing**	
2	**rest**	**ing**	
3	**wet**	**est**	
4	**sing**	**ing**	
5	**fat**	**er**	
6	**peck**	**ing**	
7	**rock**	**ed**	
8	**clap**	**ing**	
9	**hop**	**ed**	
Hint: Circle the words that end with **two consonants**			

Activity 11

Rules for suffixes

LEVEL 2

Consonants						
b	c	d	f	g	h	j
k	l	m	n	p	q	r
s	t	v	w	x	y	z

Vowels				
a	e	i	o	u

Rules for adding suffixes to words that end with a silent e:

- If the suffix starts with a <u>vowel or</u> **y**, <u>drop the</u> **e**
- If the suffix starts with a <u>consonant</u>, <u>keep the</u> **e**

	Word	Suffix	Write the new word
1	**love**	**ly**	
2	**love**	**ing**	
3	**care**	**less**	
4	**safe**	**ty**	
5	**taste**	**y**	
6	**skate**	**ed**	
7	**hate**	**ful**	
8	**prepare**	**ing**	
9	**tune**	**less**	

Hint: Circle the suffixes that start with a **vowel or y**

From: *Spotlight on Spelling*, Routledge © Glynis Hannell 2009

Activity 11

Rules for suffixes

LEVEL 3

Consonants						
b	c	d	f	g	h	j
k	l	m	n	p	q	r
s	t	v	w	x	y	z

Vowels				
a	e	i	o	u

Rules for adding suffixes to words that end with y:

- If a word ends in a <u>vowel + </u>**y**, just <u>add the suffix</u> to the word
- If a word ends in a <u>consonant + </u>**y**, <u>change</u> **y** <u>to</u> **i**

  Watch out though! There's an exception: if you add **ing** then keep the **y**

	Word	Suffix	Write the new word
1	**beauty**	**ful**	
2	**play**	**ful**	
3	**easy**	**est**	
4	**silly**	**er**	
5	**employ**	**ment**	
6	**happy**	**ness**	
7	**spy**	**ed**	
8	**spy**	**ing**	
9	**copy**	**ing**	

Hint: Circle the words that end with a **vowel + y**

Hint: Be careful with 8 and 9, they have **ing** for a suffix

Activity 12: Plurals

Teaching notes

Plurals are a special type of suffix, and there are rules governing how a word is spelt when it is pluralised.

Many spelling errors occur in pupils' work because the rules of pluralisation are not properly understood or known. In *Plurals* teachers have an opportunity to provide explicit teaching and guided practice in this skill.

However, there are also some notable exceptions to the rules in words such as *child/children*. For pupils with language-related learning difficulties, this activity can be used as a language development lesson as well as a spelling lesson, when these exception words are introduced. The steps in this activity are:

• *Step 1*
The pupils look at the singular version of the word, and at Levels 1 and 2 they also study the rule that applies. The teacher guides those pupils who need assistance, and together they look at the rules and the hint and work out the plurals. More able pupils may be able to complete the activities without the need for much assistance.

• *Step 2: Filling in the missing words*
The teacher can decide which approach is appropriate for each pupil:

– *Dictation*
This is the best approach for pupils who experience difficulties with reading and written language. For these pupils the teacher reads out each sentence and asks the pupils to fill in the missing word. The pupils can refer back to their work on the chart at the top of their page to check the spelling of the word.

– *Independent work*
This is the best approach for pupils who can cope with the reading requirements of this task easily. They are asked to work on their own, filling in the missing words as appropriate.

• *Step 3 (optional): Follow-up work*
Plural words occur over and over again in reading and spelling activities, so there will doubtless be many opportunities for teachers to provide follow-up work building on the skills introduced in this activity.

The teacher's charts needed for this activity are shown on the facing page.

Level 1

	One . . .	Lots of . . .
1	hat	hats
2	box	boxes
3	coat	coats
4	dish	dishes
5	boy	boys
6	dress	dresses
7	flag	flags
8	bunch	bunches
9	pig	pigs

Dictation (teacher's version)

1 All the **flags** were flying.
2 Sam bought two **bunches** of flowers for his mother.
3 The shop had hundreds of **hats** for sale.
4 The farmer had so many **pigs** he did not know what to do.
5 Penny needed three more **dresses** for school.
6 There were two **boys** and two girls on the bus.
7 Gordon needed a lot of **boxes** to pack away his toys.
8 The cook put all the **dishes** on the table.
9 Kim and Jim left their **coats** on the grass.

Level 2

	One . . .	Lots of . . .
1	toy	toys
2	baby	babies
3	tray	trays
4	lady	ladies
5	cowboy	cowboys
6	joey	joeys
7	pony	ponies
8	ruby	rubies
9	Sunday	Sundays

Dictation (teacher's version)

1 There were lots of **joeys** in the wildlife park.
2 Only three **babies** went to the clinic.
3 All the **cowboys** sat around the campfire.
4 The crown was made of **rubies** and diamonds.
5 All the **ponies** sheltered under the tree.
6 There are only two **Sundays** before my birthday.
7 All the **ladies** went to the office early.
8 Sam put his **toys** in the cupboard.
9 All the **trays** were on the counter of the café.

Level 3

	One . . .	Lots of . . .
1	man	men
2	child	children
3	person	people
4	mouse	mice
5	woman	women
6	sheep	sheep
7	tooth	teeth
8	deer	deer
9	cactus	cacti

Dictation (teacher's version)

1 There were many types of **cacti** on display in the garden.
2 The farmer herded all his **sheep** in from the hillside.
3 The **deer** all came in from the forest when it was cold.
4 The baby had two new **teeth**.
5 The **children** all went to school today.
6 There was a nest of **mice** in the piano.
7 The teacher asked how many **men** could help with the work.
8 There were lots of **people** at the music festival.
9 The men and **women** all waited outside the hall.

Activity 12

Plurals

LEVEL 1

Rules for adding s to most words:

- If the word ends in **x, ch, sh,** or **s,** <u>add</u> **es** to the word
- If the word ends in <u>most other letters,</u> <u>add</u> **s** to the word

	One . . .	Lots of . . .
1	**hat**	
2	**box**	
3	**coat**	
4	**dish**	
5	**boy**	
6	**dress**	
7	**flag**	
8	**bunch**	
9	**pig**	

<u>Fill in</u> the missing words.

1 All the _____ were flying.

2 Sam bought two _____ of flowers for his mother.

3 The shop had hundreds of _____ for sale.

4 The farmer had so many _____ he did not know what to do.

5 Penny needed three more _____ for school.

6 There were two _____ and two girls on the bus.

7 Gordon needed a lot of _____ to pack away his toys.

8 The cook put all the _____ on the table.

9 Kim and Jim left their _____ on the grass.

Hint: Circle the words that end with **x, ch, sh,** or **s**

From: *Spotlight on Spelling*, Routledge © Glynis Hannell 2009

Activity 12

Plurals

Rules for adding s to words that end in y:

LEVEL 2

- If the word ends in a <u>vowel + </u>**y**, <u>just add</u> **s** to the word
- If the word ends in a <u>consonant + </u>**y**, <u>change</u> **y** <u>to</u> **i** <u>and add</u> **es**

	One . . .	Lots of . . .
1	**toy**	
2	**baby**	
3	**tray**	
4	**lady**	
5	**cowboy**	
6	**joey**	
7	**pony**	
8	**ruby**	
9	**Sunday**	

<u>Fill in</u> the missing words.

1 There were lots of _____ in the wildlife park.

2 Only three _____ went to the clinic.

3 All the _____ sat around the campfire.

4 The crown was made of _____ and diamonds.

5 All the _____ sheltered under the tree.

6 There are only two _____ before my birthday.

7 All the _____ went to the office early.

8 Sam put his _____ in the cupboard.

9 All the _____ were on the counter of the café.

Hint: Circle the words that end with **consonant + y**

Activity 12

Plurals

Exception words:

Here are some exception words – their plurals do not follow the usual rules

LEVEL 3

	One . . .	Lots of . . .
1	man	
2	child	
3	person	
4	mouse	
5	woman	
6	sheep	
7	tooth	
8	deer	
9	cactus	

<u>Fill in</u> the missing words.

1 There were many types of _____ on display in the garden.

2 The farmer herded all his _____ in from the hillside.

3 The _____ all came in from the forest when it was cold.

4 The baby had two new _____.

5 The _____ all went to school today.

6 There was a nest of _____ in the piano.

7 The teacher asked how many _____ could help with the work.

8 There were lots of _____ at the music festival.

9 The men and _____ all waited outside the hall.

Hint: Say the words and listen to what sounds right

From: *Spotlight on Spelling*, Routledge © Glynis Hannell 2009

Activity 13: Compound words

Teaching notes

This *Compound words* activity is the easiest way to introduce multi-syllable words to your pupils, as it uses words that are made up of two real words with a regular spelling. Pupils are delighted to find that they can spell words such as *peanut*, *pineapple* or *hedgehog* simply by joining two easier words together.

The steps in this activity are:

• *Step 1: Copy the word*
In this activity pupils are asked to read a compound word, then 'unpack' the word into its two parts. They then write the word out in full in the last column of the chart. Of course, teacher input can be provided to give individual pupils as much help as they need. For example, some pupils may need assistance to read the word, or may need help in breaking the compound word correctly into two words.

• *Step 2: Filling in the missing words*
The teacher can decide which approach is appropriate for each pupil:

– *Dictation*
This is the best approach for pupils who experience difficulties with reading and written language. For these pupils the teacher reads out each sentence and asks the pupils to fill in the missing word. The pupils can refer back to their work on the chart at the top of their page to check the spelling of the word.
– *Independent work*
This is the best approach for pupils who can cope with the reading requirements of this task easily. They are asked to work on their own, filling in the missing words as appropriate.

• *Step 3 (optional): Follow-up work*
Compound words occur over and over again in reading and spelling activities, so there will doubtless be many opportunities for teachers to provide follow-up work building on the skills introduced in this activity.

The teacher's charts needed for this activity are shown on the following page.

Letters and sounds

Level 1

Read the word	Unpack the word	Write the word
1 popcorn	[pop][corn]	
2 peanut	[pea][nut]	
3 jigsaw	[jig][saw]	
4 cobweb	[cob][web]	
5 upset	[up][set]	
6 cowboy	[cow][boy]	
7 kidnap	[kid][nap]	
8 cupcake	[cup][cake]	
9 milkman	[milk][man]	

Dictation (teacher's version)
1 May I have a chocolate **cupcake** please?
2 Betty was very **upset** that she lost her toy.
3 The spider made a **cobweb** in the corner of the room.
4 The **cowboy** rode a big white horse.
5 We have to wait for the **milkman** to bring the milk.
6 Let's eat some **popcorn** when we watch TV.
7 I like **peanut** butter on my toast.
8 This is a hard **jigsaw**; it has 1,000 pieces.
9 I hope that they do not **kidnap** my dog.

Level 2

Read the word	Unpack the word	Write the word
1 bulldog	[bull][dog]	
2 lipstick	[lip][stick]	
3 drainpipe	[drain][pipe]	
4 pineapple	[pine][apple]	
5 downstairs	[down][stairs]	
6 spaceman	[space][man]	
7 toothpaste	[tooth][paste]	
8 overhead	[over][head]	
9 underpants	[under][pants]	

Dictation (teacher's version)
1 Beth ran **downstairs** to see if her present had come in the post.
2 Look **overhead**; there is a shooting star in the sky.
3 I like **pineapple** better than banana.
4 The actress put on her **lipstick** before she went on the stage.
5 Jack had to sleep in his **underpants** when he went camping.
6 Keep your teeth clean with **toothpaste** and a toothbrush.
7 The **bulldog** was asleep in his kennel.
8 Only one **spaceman** went outside the spacecraft.
9 The spider climbed up the **drainpipe** to keep out of the sun.

Level 3

Read the word	Unpack the word	Write the word
1 earache	[ear][ache]	
2 iceberg	[ice][berg]	
3 earthquake	[earth][quake]	
4 hedgehog	[hedge][hog]	
5 newspaper	[news][paper]	
6 hovercraft	[hover][craft]	
7 roundabout	[round][about]	
8 saucepan	[sauce][pan]	
9 screwdriver	[screw][driver]	

Dictation (teacher's version)
1 The carpenter used a **screwdriver** to fix the door.
2 The **hedgehog** came right up to the door for some milk.
3 The quickest way to cross the Channel is by **hovercraft**.
4 Hattie went to the doctor because she had an **earache**.
5 The **newspaper** had a good photograph of our school fête.
6 The chef put the **saucepan** on the stove ready to make the soup.
7 The Titanic hit an **iceberg** and sank.
8 The **roundabout** is right in the middle of the town.
9 The **earthquake** destroyed all the old buildings in the city.

Activity 13

Compound words

LEVEL 1

	Read the word	Unpack the word	Write the word
1	**popcorn**	[ ] [ ]	
2	**peanut**	[ ] [ ]	
3	**jigsaw**	[ ] [ ]	
4	**cobweb**	[ ] [ ]	
5	**upset**	[ ] [ ]	
6	**cowboy**	[ ] [ ]	
7	**kidnap**	[ ] [ ]	
8	**cupcake**	[ ] [ ]	
9	**milkman**	[ ] [ ]	

<u>Fill in</u> the missing words.

1 May I have a chocolate _____ please?

2 Betty was very _____ that she lost her toy.

3 The spider made a _____ in the corner of the room.

4 The _____ rode a big white horse.

5 We have to wait for the _____ to bring the milk.

6 Let's eat some _____ when we watch TV.

7 I like _____ butter on my toast.

8 This is a hard _____; it has 1,000 pieces.

9 I hope that they do not _____ my dog.

Activity 13

Compound words

LEVEL 2

	Read the word	Unpack the word	Write the word
1	**bulldog**	[ ] [ ]	
2	**lipstick**	[ ] [ ]	
3	**drainpipe**	[ ] [ ]	
4	**pineapple**	[ ] [ ]	
5	**downstairs**	[ ] [ ]	
6	**spaceman**	[ ] [ ]	
7	**toothpaste**	[ ] [ ]	
8	**overhead**	[ ] [ ]	
9	**underpants**	[ ] [ ]	

<u>Fill in</u> the missing words.

1   Beth ran _____ to see if her present had come in the post.

2   Look _____; there is a shooting star in the sky.

3   I like _____ better than banana.

4   The actress put on her _____ before she went on the stage.

5   Jack had to sleep in his _____ when he went camping.

6   Keep your teeth clean with _____ and a toothbrush.

7   The _____ was asleep in his kennel.

8   Only one _____ went outside the spacecraft.

9   The spider climbed up the _____ to keep out of the sun.

   From: *Spotlight on Spelling*, Routledge © Glynis Hannell 2009

Activity 13

Compound words

LEVEL 3

	Read the word	Unpack the word	Write the word
1	**earache**	[ ] [ ]	
2	**iceberg**	[ ] [ ]	
3	**earthquake**	[ ] [ ]	
4	**hedgehog**	[ ] [ ]	
5	**newspaper**	[ ] [ ]	
6	**hovercraft**	[ ] [ ]	
7	**roundabout**	[ ] [ ]	
8	**saucepan**	[ ] [ ]	
9	**screwdriver**	[ ] [ ]	

<u>Fill in</u> the missing words.

1   The carpenter used a _____ to fix the door.

2   The _____ came right up to the door for some milk.

3   The quickest way to cross the Channel is by _____.

4   Hattie went to the doctor because she had an _____.

5   The _____ had a good photograph of our school fête.

6   The chef put the _____ on the stove ready to make the soup.

7   The Titanic hit an _____ and sank.

8   The _____ is right in the middle of the town.

9   The _____ destroyed all the old buildings in the city.

CHAPTER 4

Tough words

Exceptions to the rules

Regular words that follow a phonic pattern should *always* be taught by sounding out and the use of regular phonic spelling. Phonic words are the easiest spelling patterns to learn. When a pupil learns a phonically regular word, the next time they try to spell that word, they can 'reconstruct' it, using a combination of memory and their skills in sounding out. For example, the pupil may remember that *shout* is part of the *ou* family and, from there, be able to build the word without having actually to recall all the letters.

However, the English language contains many tough or *exception* words and these are not nearly as easy to learn as phonically regular words.

Exception words have to be recalled in their entirety. In fact, attempts to reconstruct the word using a combination of sounds and recalled spelling can create all sorts of problems! The phonic patterns interfere with the correct spelling and the pupils produce words such as *throogh*, *tougff* or *arnswer*. Sometimes it is easy to assume that the pupils have simply been lazy or inattentive when they produce such incorrect spellings. However, close inspection of their attempts will often show that they have taken considerable time and trouble, even though the results are so disappointing.

Exception words go against anticipated spelling patterns with no apparent rhyme or reason! How come *they* sounds just like *hay*, *day*, *may or play*, but has a different spelling pattern? Why don't we spell *friend* the same way as *mend*, *bend* or *lend*? For young learners, such inconsistencies can confuse and frustrate. The pupils may have gained confidence in spelling regular words, only to be confronted with words that do not obey the rules.

In this situation, rote learning simply has to be used. Words that have arbitrary, unpredictable spelling patterns can only be remembered if they are painstakingly learned by heart. Rote learning is the hardest form of learning and should be reserved for exception words, where no other option exists.

Almost all pupils will need to put in extra effort to master the exception words in the English language. They may learn words quite well and recall them successfully during the weekly spelling test. However, when new words are introduced, the previous words are lost and the cycle begins all over again.

Because these spelling patterns do not make sense, pupils are forced to rely much more on *memory*. Unfortunately, memory-based learning decays very rapidly without continuous reinforcement, and this may especially apply to pupils who have learning difficulties. Pupils will vary in how difficult they find it to learn exception words, and how much teacher support they will need. Some pupils will experience a 'learn and forget' cycle over and over again.

Certainly, continuous reinforcement will help your pupils to spell exception words successfully. However, this process can be supplemented by activities that involve learning through different modalities and this is called *multisensory learning*.

- **Thinking and talking** helps pupils to gain familiarity with exception words. The process also helps to engage the pupils' interest and encourages them to *code* the information about a spelling pattern in a new format. For example, a pupil may notice that she can use *a [pie]ce of pie* to remember how to spell *piece*. Or she may recite the letters over and over again to create a verbal patter for a word such as *they*: *T-H-E-Y spells they, P-L-A-Y spells play*. However, beware! Many pupils with memory difficulties forget mnemonics and verbal patter just as quickly as they forget how to spell a word!

- **Looking and visualising** helps pupils to remember and replicate the look of a word when the word will not 'sound out'. This is much more difficult for some pupils than others. However, being able to recognise when a word *looks right* is an important part of spelling and proofreading, so a focus on recognising the appearance of a correct spelling is helpful.

- **Feeling and moving** helps some pupils to remember a spelling. As the fingers follow a repeated pattern, the movement becomes automatic. We can call this *motor memory*. Writing and rewriting, or typing the same words over and over again, will help to consolidate the learning more effectively than simply saying the letters over and over. *Rainbow writing* (over-writing a word time and time again with different colours) or *tactile writing* (tracing words into sand or wet paint, etc.) can also really help some pupils to literally 'get the feel' of a spelling pattern.

Activity 14: Think about spelling (1)

Teaching notes

Research has shown that careful visual preview and inspection of irregular words assists pupils in learning how to spell those words. We also know that active thinking, discrimination and analysis of the spelling patterns further a pupil's familiarity with the correct spelling pattern. Learning *how* to learn is an intrinsic part of *Think about spelling (1)* and helps all pupils (good spellers and poor spellers) to develop good strategies.

This activity has a topic for group discussion (see below). This does not appear on the pupils' worksheets, but is an important part of the exercise.

The steps in this activity are:

• *Step 1: Match the word and write it down*
First, the pupils look at the correct spelling and find two more examples of the correct spelling in the same row of the chart. They then write the correct spelling down. Even pupils with very poor spelling skills usually find this easy, as the recognition, matching and copying of spelling patterns is much easier than remembering spelling. But this activity does exercise the pupil's ability to visualise the word and begins to lay good foundations for more advanced learning.

• *Step 2: Check the sentences*
The pupils now check sentences and look at the target words they have been learning.

Correct words are ticked and incorrect words are corrected by the pupils. This provides good consolidation of previous learning and trains the pupils to proofread carefully, using visualisation of the correct word pattern as a reference point.

Group discussion topic
Why is the correct spelling 'tricky' to spell?

Pupils with better reading and spelling skills may lead the way in this part of the activity. They may say something like:

> You think 'one' starts with the 'w' sound, but it doesn't, it starts with 'o'.

or

> 'You' has the 'ou' sound like 'out', so you think it will say 'yow', but it doesn't, it says 'yoo.'

This is an important part of the activity, as *thinking* and *talking* about spelling patterns helps to shift the learning from memory to understanding mode.

Of course, the teacher will also make teaching points to help pupils to notice and remember these 'tricky' words. This is good modelling of how to *think* about spelling patterns and a valuable learning for everyone in the group.

There are no teacher's charts for this activity.

Activity 14

Think about spelling (1)

LEVEL 1

	Correct spelling	Circle the words that have the right spelling			Write the correct spelling here
1	**are**	are	ar	are	
2	**you**	you	yuo	you	
3	**said**	said	said	sed	
4	**were**	were	weer	were	
5	**do**	do	doo	do	
6	**they**	they	they	thay	
7	**one**	wun	one	one	
8	**two**	tow	two	two	
9	**who**	how	who	who	

Look at the underlined words below and tick the words that are right. Write the correct word above each mistake.

1 Thay had two boys and wun girl in their boat.

2 'Who will hold the rope? How will hold the tent?' sed Dad.

3 You are a funny boy; ar you going to be a clown?

4 Do they like chocolate or doo thay like peanuts best?

5 I said that I like peanuts; Dad sed that he likes chocolate.

6 'I am going to the zoo; aer you coming too?' said Kane.

7 They were going to the shops and then thay weer going home.

8 'Do you want one or tow bananas?' sed Sam.

9 We were very cold but we weer having fun in the snow.

Activity 14

Think about spelling (1)

LEVEL 2

	Correct spelling	Circle the words that have the right spelling			Write the correct spelling here
1	would	would	wold	would	
2	only	only	only	onely	
3	water	water	warter	water	
4	other	uther	other	other	
5	their	theyr	their	their	
6	once	wunce	once	once	
7	walk	walk	worlk	walk	
8	eyes	eyes	eyes	ieys	
9	four	four	foure	four	

Look at the underlined words below and tick the words that are right. Write the correct word above each mistake.

1   I onely go swimming if the water is warm.

2   The other animals went into theyr den when it rained.

3   I would like to see the uther side of the world.

4   Wunce I dropped my hat in the warter.

5   The other day four of my friends went for a worlk in the park.

6   They could not believe their ieys when they saw four elephants in the yard.

7   You can only go to the circus wunce with this ticket.

8   Theyr mother gave them some water to play in.

9   Wold you like to shut your ieys?

Activity 14

Think about spelling (1)

LEVEL 3

	Correct spelling	Circle the words that have the right spelling			Write the correct spelling here
1	**hour**	howr	hour	hour	
2	**tongue**	tongue	tongue	tonge	
3	**answer**	answer	answer	answere	
4	**money**	money	moniy	money	
5	**listened**	lissened	listened	listened	
6	**building**	biulding	building	building	
7	**laugh**	laugh	laugh	larf	
8	**people**	people	poeple	people	
9	**exhibition**	exhibition	exibition	exhibition	

Look at the underlined words below and tick the words that are right. Write the correct word above each mistake.

1 The poeple waited for an hour to get into the exibition.

2 The building cost a lot of moniy because it was on an island.

3 The lizard's tonge was blue.

4 I heard the people laugh when I lissened at the door.

5 The doctor looked at the boy's tonge and listened to his chest.

6 The people waited an howr for the answer to their question.

7 I hope they won't larf if I give the wrong answere.

8 The exibition was in a very large biulding in the town.

9 The people lissened to the music for an howr.

From: *Spotlight on Spelling*, Routledge © Glynis Hannell 2009

Activity 15: Think about spelling (2)

Teaching notes

This is the second *Think about spelling* activity. Once again, pupils are asked to look at the correct spelling of the word and match it with other, correct spelling patterns and then write it down. This helps to build the pupils' familiarity with the appearance of the word. Research has shown that careful visual preview and inspection of irregular words assists pupils in learning how to spell them. The process of copying the correct word down further consolidates their familiarity with the word.

This activity also has a topic for group discussion (see below). This does not appear on the pupils' worksheets, but is an important part of the exercise.

The steps in this activity are:

• *Step 1: Match the word and write it down*
First, the pupils look at the correct spelling and find two more examples of the correct spelling in the same row of the chart. They then write the correct spelling down. Even pupils with very poor spelling skills usually find this easy, as the recognition, matching and copying of spelling patterns is much easier than remembering spelling. But this activity does begin to lay good foundations for more advanced learning.

• *Step 2: Check the sentences*
The pupils now check sentences and look at the target words they have been learning. Correct words are ticked and incorrect words are corrected by the pupils. This provides good consolidation of previous learning and trains the pupils to proofread carefully. Having to decide whether a spelling is right or not promotes good word discrimination skills; the pupils cannot assume that every target word is written incorrectly. This makes them think carefully before they correct!

Group discussion topic
What is wrong with the odd one out?

Pupils can be asked to talk about what is wrong with the 'odd one out' (that is, the incorrect spelling). Such discussion helps all pupils to develop a clear picture of the correct way to spell a word. Many pupils will not initially realise that spelling patterns can be looked at, talked about and compared. Group or class discussions will help these pupils to develop skills in looking at words as impartial observers. This is a good basis for successful learning. For example, pupils may say something like:

But 'any' starts with 'a' and that word starts with 'e'.

or

The 'e' is in the wrong place; it has to go at the end of 'are'.

This deliberate comparison of the correct versus incorrect spelling helps to familiarise the pupil with the word, making them feel something of an expert on the way to spell it!

There are no teacher's charts for this activity.

Activity 15

Think about spelling (2)

LEVEL 1

	Correct spelling	Circle the words that have the right spelling			Write the correct spelling here
1	**love**	luv	love	love	
2	**school**	school	school	shool	
3	**any**	any	eny	any	
4	**know**	know	now	know	
5	**put**	put	put	poot	
6	**friend**	frend	friend	friend	
7	**have**	hav	have	have	
8	**find**	find	fiend	find	
9	**want**	want	want	wont	

Look at the underlined words below and tick the words that are right. Write the correct word above each mistake.

1   I <u>love</u> going to <u>shool</u> with my <u>frend</u>.

2   I <u>now</u> I <u>have</u> to <u>find</u> a toy for my <u>friend</u>.

3   I <u>want</u> to <u>hav</u> a party for my birthday.

4   Do you <u>know eny</u> good songs?

5   <u>Have</u> you <u>poot</u> your name down at <u>school</u> for sports day?

6   I <u>want</u> a banana; I <u>luv</u> bananas and I <u>luv</u> apples.

7   Did you <u>fiend</u> any kids at <u>shool</u>?

8   <u>Put</u> the dog in the box; I <u>want</u> to take him to <u>school</u>.

9   Can you <u>find</u> any biscuits? I <u>wont</u> one.

Activity 15

Think about spelling (2)

LEVEL 2

	Correct spelling	Circle the words that have the right spelling			Write the correct spelling here
1	**castle**	casel	castle	castle	
2	**son**	son	sun	son	
3	**earth**	earth	earth	erth	
4	**own**	owne	own	own	
5	**half**	half	haff	half	
6	**work**	work	work	werk	
7	**dinosaur**	dinosaur	dynosor	dinosaur	
8	**choir**	cwire	choir	choir	
9	**deaf**	deff	deaf	deaf	

Look at the underlined words below and tick the words that are right. Write the correct word above each mistake.

1 The king gave his <u>sun</u> a toy <u>castle</u>.

2 Zac did the <u>werk</u> on his <u>own</u>.

3 You have to dig deep in the <u>erth</u> to find <u>dinosaur</u> bones.

4 The <u>dinosur</u> was <u>half deff</u>, so he did not hear the thunder.

5 The <u>cwire</u> sang one song and then Hayley sang on her <u>own</u>.

6 Dad gave <u>haff</u> the cake to his <u>son</u> and <u>haff</u> to his daughter.

7 It is hard <u>work</u> building a <u>casel</u>.

8 <u>Half</u> the <u>choir</u> were boys and <u>haff</u> the <u>cwire</u> were girls.

9 If you are <u>deaf</u> you may need to sit close to hear the <u>cwire</u> sing.

Activity 15

Think about spelling (2)

LEVEL 3

	Correct spelling	Circle the words that have the right spelling			Write the correct spelling here
1	**island**	island	iland	island	
2	**height**	hyight	height	height	
3	**onions**	unions	onions	onions	
4	**veins**	veins	vanes	veins	
5	**blood**	blood	blood	blud	
6	**sword**	sword	sord	sword	
7	**canoe**	canoe	canoo	canoe	
8	**guess**	guess	guess	gess	
9	**soldier**	soljure	soldier	soldier	

Look at the underlined words below and tick the words that are right. Write the correct word above each mistake.

1   Blood runs through your vanes and arteries.

2   The survivors paddled a canoo to the island.

3   You could guess he was a soljure because he had a sord.

4   I would gess the hyight of the tree was about 30 metres.

5   The soldier had unions and cheese in his sandwich.

6   Unions taste good when they are cooked.

7   The soljure was the same height as the door.

8   They had to guess where the canoo was on the iland.

9   A nurse might inject vaccinations into blud veins.

From: *Spotlight on Spelling*, Routledge © Glynis Hannell 2009   **81**

Activity 16: Silent letters

Teaching notes

Silent letters often confuse young learners, who try to stay with sounds that they can hear when they write. Who would guess that *knee* started with a *k*, or that *lamb* ends with a *b*?

In *Silent letters* the pupils are asked to pick out the silent letter in the word and then copy the word down, highlighting the silent letter again. This helps them to think about the spelling and notice the silent letter. Finally, they are asked to write the word from memory and then insert the word into sentences. This is so that they begin to become accustomed to *writing* the word for themselves both out of context and in context.

The teacher's charts for this activity are shown below.

Level 1

1 Your hair is a mess; get your **comb**.
2 The mother sheep looked for her little **lamb**.
3 Missie is a chatterbox; she can **talk** all day.
4 Sally hurt her **knee** when she fell over.
5 I will cut the cake in **half**.
6 I will count one, **two**, three and then pull out your loose tooth.
7 Do you know **when** the shop will open?
8 You must **write** to Grandad to say thank you for the present.
9 **Why** have you got your red boots on?

Level 2

1 Look at your **watch** and tell me the time.
2 If you don't know the answer you can **guess**.
3 A penguin is black and **white**.
4 Do you **listen** to music in the car?
5 Do you **know** how to swim?
6 There is sometimes a **sign** that says EXIT.
7 You can eat a **biscuit** if you are hungry.
8 The day after Tuesday is **Wednesday**.
9 It would be very difficult to **climb** Everest.

Level 3

1 Rod played an electric **guitar** in the band.
2 **Autumn** is the time of year when bears begin to hibernate.
3 We had to stay indoors for a **whole** week because of the snow.
4 Make sure you **fasten** the tent on to the car roof properly.
5 You have to be **honest** when the police interview you.
6 The girl put on her **badge** to show that she was a guide.
7 The **salmon** swam up the river to the place where they were born.
8 It is good to be able to speak a **foreign** language when you travel.
9 Firemen sometimes have to go into a burning **building**.

Level 1

	Word	Silent letter
1	knee	k
2	lamb	b
3	why	h
4	comb	b
5	half	l
6	two	w
7	when	h
8	talk	l
9	write	w

Level 2

	Word	Silent letter
1	biscuit	u
2	listen	t
3	climb	b
4	watch	t
5	sign	g
6	white	h
7	know	k
8	Wednesday	d
9	guess	u

Level 3

	Word	Silent letter
1	honest	h
2	badge	d
3	guitar	u
4	autumn	n
5	building	u
6	salmon	l
7	whole	w
8	fasten	t
9	foreign	g

Activity 16

Silent letters

LEVEL 1

	Read the word and highlight the silent letter	Copy the word and highlight the silent letter	Cover the word and write it from memory	Cover the word and write it from memory
1	**knee**			
2	**lamb**			
3	**why**			
4	**comb**			
5	**half**			
6	**two**			
7	**when**			
8	**talk**			
9	**write**			

Fill in the missing words.

1 Your hair is a mess; get your _____.

2 The mother sheep looked for her little _____.

3 Missie is a chatterbox; she can _____ all day.

4 Sally hurt her _____ when she fell over.

5 I will cut the cake in _____.

6 I will count one, _____, three and then pull out your loose tooth.

7 Do you know _____ the shop will open?

8 You must _____ to Grandad to say thank you for the present.

9 _____ have you got your red boots on?

From: *Spotlight on Spelling*, Routledge © Glynis Hannell 2009

Activity 16

Silent letters

LEVEL 2

	Read the word and highlight the silent letter	Copy the word and highlight the silent letter	Cover the word and write it from memory	Cover the word and write it from memory
1	biscuit			
2	listen			
3	climb			
4	watch			
5	sign			
6	white			
7	know			
8	Wednesday			
9	guess			

Fill in the missing words.

1 Look at your _____ and tell me the time.

2 If you don't know the answer you can _____ .

3 A penguin is black and _____ .

4 Do you _____ to music in the car?

5 Do you _____ how to swim?

6 There is sometimes a _____ that says EXIT.

7 You can eat a _____ if you are hungry.

8 The day after Tuesday is _____ .

9 It would be very difficult to _____ Everest.

Activity 16

Silent letters

LEVEL 3

	Read the word and highlight the silent letter	Copy the word and highlight the silent letter	Cover the word and write it from memory	Cover the word and write it from memory
1	honest			
2	badge			
3	guitar			
4	autumn			
5	building			
6	salmon			
7	whole			
8	fasten			
9	foreign			

<u>Fill in</u> the missing words.

1   Rod played an electric _____ in the band.

2   _____ is the time of year when bears begin to hibernate.

3   We had to stay indoors for a _____ week because of the snow.

4   Make sure you _____ the tent on to the car roof properly.

5   You have to be _____ when the police interview you.

6   The girl put on her _____ to show that she was a guide.

7   The _____ swam up the river to the place where they were born.

8   It is good to be able to speak a _____ language when you travel.

9   Firemen sometimes have to go into a burning _____.

   From: *Spotlight on Spelling*, Routledge   © Glynis Hannell 2009

Activity 17: Amazing words

Teaching notes

Many exception words are very frustrating for pupils to learn. Words such as *the*, *your*, *where*, *one*, *who*, *were*, *there* and *was* are dull and yet need to be used (and spelt correctly) day after day. It is easy for adults to think that, because these words are used so often, they are easy to spell. Nothing could be further from the truth!

The easiest words to learn to spell or read have

- a distinctive visual appearance,
- an interesting meaning and
- a regular phonic spelling.

Many pupils and their teachers become very disheartened when the pupils continually experience problems in spelling short, simple words that seem as if they should be so easy. As one exasperated teacher said,

I can't see what he does not understand about 't-h-e spells the'!

Amazing words introduces spellings that have

- a distinctive visual appearance and
- an interesting meaning,

but that do not necessarily have

- a regular phonic spelling.

These words will give pupils a boost of confidence. Imagine being able to spell *tyrannosaurus rex* (even if you are still having trouble with *why*, *because* or *though*!).

Popular children's names are included in this activity. Teachers may like to extend this aspect and teach the spelling of *all* the names in the class.

Some of the words, such as *Egypt* and *tsunami*, may not be familiar to the pupils, even though the spelling is fun to learn, so some discussion on word meanings is also helpful.

There are no teacher's charts for this activity.

Activity 17

Amazing words

LEVEL 1

	Read the sentence	Copy the **bold** word	Copy the **bold** word again
1	The big, bad **wolf** tricked Little Red Riding Hood.		
2	**Pluto** is a dwarf planet.		
3	An **emu** is a very big bird that cannot fly.		
4	**Ethan** likes to skateboard.		
5	You can buy a **hotdog** at the shopping centre.		
6	**Emily** has a pet dog.		
7	Mum put a **picnic** in the basket.		
8	Sam loves to eat **pizza** with cheese.		
9	Zac sat on a **banana** and squashed it.		

Answer these questions using the words you have learnt.

1 Who has a pet dog? _____.

2 Who tricked Little Red Riding Hood? _____.

3 What is the name of a big bird that cannot fly? _____.

4 What does Sam like to eat? _____.

5 What is the dwarf planet called? _____.

6 Who likes to skateboard? _____.

7 What did Mum put in the basket? _____.

8 What did Zac sit on and squash? _____.

9 What can you buy at the shopping centre? _____.

    From: *Spotlight on Spelling*, Routledge © Glynis Hannell 2009

Activity 17

Amazing words

LEVEL 2

	Read the sentence	Copy the **bold** word	Copy the **bold** word again
1	A **dolphin** is a very intelligent sea animal.		
2	**Chloe** likes to swim in the sea.		
3	A **gorilla** eats plants and insects.		
4	Ben's favourite Italian food is **spaghetti**.		
5	**John** has a pet snake.		
6	A **doughnut** has sugar on the outside.		
7	The **triceratops** was a plant-eating dinosaur.		
8	A **volcano** can erupt and throw out rocks.		
9	There are pyramids in **Egypt**.		

Answer these questions using the words you have learnt.

1 Who likes to swim in the sea? _____.

2 What is Ben's favourite Italian food? _____.

3 Where are the pyramids? _____.

4 What throws out rocks? _____.

5 Which animal eats plants and insects? _____.

6 Who has a pet snake? _____.

7 Which sea animal is very intelligent? _____.

8 What has sugar on the outside? _____.

9 Which dinosaur ate plants? _____.

Activity 17

Amazing words

LEVEL 3

	Read the sentence	Copy the **bold** word	Copy the **bold** word again
1	**Nicholas** joined the Sea Scouts last week.		
2	The longest river in the USA is the **Mississippi**.		
3	Kaleb goes to **tae kwon do** on Fridays.		
4	The **tyrannosaurus rex** was a meat-eating dinosaur.		
5	The **hippopotamus** is a dangerous African animal.		
6	A **tsunami** is a wave caused by an earthquake.		
7	**Phoebe** is the fastest runner in Brighton.		
8	The **alligator** overturned Frank's canoe.		
9	Mrs Biddle was bitten by a **mosquito**.		

Answer these questions using the words you have learnt.

1 Who is the fastest runner in Brighton? _____.

2 What is the name of a meat-eating dinosaur? _____.

3 Where does Kaleb go on Fridays? _____.

4 What is the longest river in the USA? _____.

5 Which dangerous animal lives in Africa? _____.

6 Which animal overturned Frank's canoe? _____.

7 Who joined the Sea Scouts last week? _____.

8 What was Mrs Biddle bitten by? _____.

9 What do we call a wave caused by an earthquake? _____.

   From: *Spotlight on Spelling*, Routledge © Glynis Hannell 2009

Activity 18: Important words

Teaching notes

There are some words that, although not featured in lists of high-frequency words, are nonetheless important for pupils to master. Such words include days of the week, months of the year and the names of continents and oceans.

Some of the words in these sets have regular, phonetic spelling, while others do not. The tasks in *Important words* will give your pupils the chance to look at these words, notice special characteristics about them and become familiar with the letters that they contain.

For example, the younger or less able pupils work first with days of the week. Working out which days have an *o* in them, or a *u*, helps to build up their awareness of the quite difficult spelling patterns for Monday, Tuesday and Thursday.

Similarly, at the other levels the pupils also have to notice spelling features, such as months of the year that contain three *e*s or continents of the world that start with *two vowels*.

If pupils find it difficult to remember how to spell these words, extra practice can of course be given.

Some words are regular and, if this is so, an emphasis on working with the phonic pattern will be the best way to teach the spelling. For example, *Sunday*, *March*, *May* or even *Atlantic* lend themselves to being taught by breaking up the words into sounds and then writing down the appropriate letters.

On the other hand, words such as *Wednesday*, *February* or *Europe* are not regular phonic words and will best be taught by other methods. Activities 20 and 21 in the following chapter provide spelling practice charts that may be useful. Talking about unusual spelling patterns can also help pupils learn how to spell them.

There are no teacher's charts for this activity.

Activity 18

Important words

LEVEL 1

	Days of the week	Copy the word	Copy the word again
1	**Monday**		
2	**Tuesday**		
3	**Wednesday**		
4	**Thursday**		
5	**Friday**		
6	**Saturday**		
7	**Sunday**		

Fill in the missing letters

1 M _ n d _ y   Th _ r _ d _ y

2 T _ e s d a _   W _ d _ e s _ a y

3 We _ n e s _ a y   Mo _ d _ y

4 T _ u r _ d a _   Fr _ d _ y

5 F _ i _ a y   Su _ d a _

6 Sat _ r _ a y   Tu _ s _ a _

7 S _ n d _ a y   S _ t u _ d _ y

Answer these questions

1 Which days have **o** in their name?

2 Which days have **s** in their name?

3 Which days have **u** in their name?

4 Which days have **r** in their name?

5 Which days have **six** letters in their name?

6 Which day has the **most** letters?

From: *Spotlight on Spelling*, Routledge © Glynis Hannell 2009

Activity 18

Important words

LEVEL 2

	Months of the year	Copy the word	Copy the word again
1	**January**		
2	**February**		
3	**March**		
4	**April**		
5	**May**		
6	**June**		
7	**July**		
8	**August**		
9	**September**		
10	**October**		
11	**November**		
12	**December**		

Fill in the missing letters

1 J _ n _ ary   Ma _   Se _ te _ be _
2 F _ bru _ ry   J _ n _   _ ct _ ber
3 Ma _ c _   J _ ly   N _ ve _ b _ r
4 A _ ri _   A _ g _ st   D _ ce _ b _ r

Answer these questions

1 Which months have **o** in their name?

2 Which months have **u** in their name?

3 Which months have **three e**'s in their name?

4 Which months start with a **vowel**?

5 Which months end with **y**?

6 Which month has a **g** in its name?

From: *Spotlight on Spelling*, Routledge © Glynis Hannell 2009

Activity 18

Important words

LEVEL 3

	Continents and oceans	Copy the word	Copy the word again
1	**Europe**		
2	**America**		
3	**Asia**		
4	**Oceania**		
5	**Antarctica**		
6	**Australia**		
7	**Africa**		
8	**Pacific Ocean**		
9	**Atlantic Ocean**		
10	**Arctic Ocean**		
11	**Indian Ocean**		
12	**Southern Ocean**		

Answer these questions

1 Which continents have names starting with **A**?

2 Which continent <u>does not</u> end with **a**?

3 Which continents have **c** in their name?

4 Which continents have **u** in their name?

5 Which continents have **r** in their name?

6 Which continents have names that start with **two vowels**?

7 Which oceans have names ending with **c**?

8 Which oceans have names ending with **n**?

9 Which oceans have names starting with **A**?

10 Which oceans have names that start with **three consonants**?

11 Which ocean does not have **a** in its name?

12 Which ocean contains the name of a country?

Activity 19: Homophones

Teaching notes

Homophones are two or more words that sound alike but that mean something different, and usually have a different spelling. Each spelling can be regular, or one or both may be irregular.

The pupils are provided with some good scaffolding to help them complete *Homophones*, but, as with all the activities in this book, teacher input is important to ensure that every pupil gets the most out of the learning opportunity.

The steps in this activity are:

- *Step 1: Read the sentences and find pairs of homophones*
Many pupils will benefit from being able to read the sentences with support from the teacher or a peer. The sentences all contain two homophones and the pupils are asked to pick the pair from the other words in

the sentence. First, they should circle the words in the sentence and then write them both down in the next column. Because both homophones are embedded in a meaningful sentence, the pupils will usually be able to deduce the meaning of each word.

- *Step 2: Find the right word*
The pupils move to the second chart on the page. This has clues for one word from each pair of the homophones. The clues are in the same order as the sentences in the original chart, so the pupils only need to refer back to the first chart and select one word from the pair they have previously written down for that item number. Some pupils may need assistance to read or interpret the clues.

There are no teacher's charts for this activity.

Activity 19

Homophones

LEVEL 1

<u>Read</u> the sentence and circle the <u>two words</u> that <u>sound</u> the same.
<u>Write</u> the two words down.

1 I would like to be a bee.   _____ _____

2 I bought four roses for my mother.   _____ _____

3 We can see the sea.   _____ _____

4 The poor dog had cut his paw.   _____ _____

5 The bear had a bare head.   _____ _____

6 I knew I had a new book to read.   _____ _____

7 The two boys went to the zoo.   _____ _____

8 Has the bean been cooked yet?   _____ _____

9 Which girl is dressed up as the witch? _____ _____

Which one of your two words matches the clue? <u>Write</u> it down.

1 An insect   _____

2 A number   _____

3 Something made of water   _____

4 Means sad or unlucky   _____

5 An animal   _____

6 Not old   _____

7 A number   _____

8 A vegetable   _____

9 A woman with black clothes   _____

Activity 19

Homophones

LEVEL 2

<u>Read</u> the sentence and circle the <u>two words</u> that <u>sound</u> the same.
Write the two words down.

1   The lion gave a loud roar when he saw
    the raw meat.   _____ _____

2   Don't stare at the man on the stair.   _____ _____

3   The robbers tried to steal the steel.   _____ _____

4   Sam rode his bike on the road.   _____ _____

5   George sent Isobelle some scent.   _____ _____

6   I have to warn you, the carpet is
    worn out.   _____ _____

7   I would like to walk in the wood.   _____ _____

8   The knight left the castle at dead of
    night.   _____ _____

9   She used flour for the cake and put a
    flower on the top.   _____ _____

Which one of your two words matches the clue? <u>Write</u> it down.

1   An animal noise   _____

2   A way of looking   _____

3   A metal   _____

4   A place to drive   _____

5   This smells nice   _____

6   Very old   _____

7   A place with trees   _____

8   When it is dark   _____

9   Something that grows in the garden _____

From: *Spotlight on Spelling*, Routledge © Glynis Hannell 2009

Activity 19

Homophones

LEVEL 3

Read the sentence and circle the two words that sound the same.
Write the two words down.

1 He wore his uniform to the war. _____ _____

2 I will slay the wolf and then escape on my sleigh. _____ _____

3 The whole team crawled through the hole. _____ _____

4 The thief was caught and had to go to court. _____ _____

5 Take a piece of pie and leave me in peace. _____ _____

6 Jack missed the path in the mist. _____ _____

7 You are not allowed to talk aloud in here. _____ _____

8 I guessed that she was the guest of honour. _____ _____

9 The king was thrown off his throne. _____ _____

Which one of your two words matches the clue? Write it down.

1 A battle _____

2 A way of travelling in snow _____

3 A gap or space _____

4 Where a judge sits _____

5 Quietness _____

6 Fog or cloud _____

7 Not whispering _____

8 Someone who is invited _____

9 A place where a king sits _____

From: *Spotlight on Spelling*, Routledge © Glynis Hannell 2009

CHAPTER 5

Mixed challenges

A miscellany

This is the final chapter of *Spotlight on Spelling*. It contains a variety of activities that you, as the teacher, may find useful as supplementary spelling activities for your pupils.

Commonly used words (Activity 20) gives you the opportunity to check each pupil's grasp of the most everyday words. This can be used and reused as often as you like, so that you can identify each pupil's spelling strengths and areas of difficulties and plan an individual programme. You can also gain an overview of how the whole class is coping with these essential words. Progress can be tracked by using the check at intervals throughout the school year.

Spelling tricks (Activity 21) is a very useful activity in which you can ask your pupils to try out various strategies for learning to spell a word. Individual pupils vary in the way they learn best, and this activity gives the pupils a chance to experiment with several different ways and to talk about how helpful they found them. Taking an objective, thoughtful look at your own learning is a very powerful teacher.

Anagrams (Activity 22) introduces your pupils to the skill of reorganising letters into new patterns to make different words. Their word knowledge and inventiveness will be put to the test as they attempt to make as many words as possible.

In *Twisters* (Activity 23), the sentences can be used for discussion, dictation or both. Rather like the spelling equivalent of tongue twisters, there are some very tricky words to write, but lots of fun as pupils discover just how frustrating some spelling can be!

Learn your own words (Activity 24) is a worksheet on which pupils can practise learning words taken from their own written work. It is based on the *look–cover–write–check* approach, with an important addition. The pupils are asked to copy the word down on to the chart and then *learn it your own way*. This means that each pupil is being asked to activate their own preferred learning strategies, which they may have discovered during *Spelling tricks* (Activity 21). Teachers may like to remind pupils of the various options they have.

Finally, *Seven in a row* (Activity 25) is a more intensive approach to learning how to spell. Once again, the pupils select words taken from their own writing. For many pupils with spelling difficulties this method, spread over a period of at least seven days, is a much better way to learn spelling than a single session of learning.

Activity 20: Commonly used words

Teaching notes

It makes sense to ensure that your pupils can spell the words they are most likely to use. In particular, pupils who have difficulty in learning to spell should not have to learn words that they are unlikely to use in the near future. The best learning outcomes are achieved when a pupil learns to spell a word and then uses that word time and time again in their own daily writing.

Commonly used words allows you and your pupils to see how many such words they can spell. Some words are regular and some are irregular. Level 1 introduces words that are the most commonly used, but remember that this does not mean they are the easiest to spell!

Teachers can use these sets of checklists (ten words per set) in a variety of ways. For example, you can:

- identify words that an individual pupil cannot yet spell, as a basis for an individual programme;
- identify words that a group of pupils cannot yet spell, as a basis for a group programme;
- identify pupils who are ready to move on to more challenging words;
- use the checklists at intervals to track pupils' progress.

The words are presented in sets of ten. There is room for the teacher to mark the sheet so that it can be used as a pupil or teacher reference. Many pupils benefit from having their personal record sheets on the desk as they write. They can double-check words that they can usually spell but where they are not 100 per cent certain, and can refer to the chart for help with spelling a word that is not yet within their repertoire.

Teachers may like to highlight one or two words that a pupil has not yet mastered and nominate these as 'target words'. The challenge to the pupil is:

> Can you do all your writing work for a whole week without making any mistakes on these words? If you can, your reward will be . . .

This means that the pupil is motivated to check and spell these words correctly in their daily work, and in doing so is likely to learn to spell the words as they write.

Many pupils will need constant reinforcement to encourage them to persevere with their list of 100 words. Teachers may like to cut the sheet into sections, so that a pupil is only faced with, say, one or two sets of words at any one time. When a pupil can spell all 100 words at any level it's certainly time to celebrate! Make sure that your pupils enjoy a sense of achievement when they have completed a set or a whole level.

There are no teacher's charts for this activity.

Activity 20

Commonly used words

LEVEL 1

Set 1		Set 2		Set 3		Set 4		Set 5	
a		are		at		all		an	
and		as		be		but		do	
in		for		by		can		five	
is		he		from		not		each	
it		his		had		said		how	
of		I		have		we		if	
that		on		one		were		she	
the		they		or		what		their	
to		was		this		when		use	
you		with		word		your		which	

Set 6		Set 7		Set 8		Set 9		Set 10	
about		has		could		been		come	
many		her		go		call		day	
other		him		more		find		did	
out		into		my		first		down	
so		like		no		long		get	
some		look		number		now		made	
them		make		people		oil		may	
then		time		see		than		over	
these		two		way		water		part	
up		would		write		who		will	

Activity 20

Commonly used words

LEVEL 2

Set 11		Set 12		Set 13		Set 14		Set 15	
know		after		before		any		also	
little		back		good		boy		around	
live		give		help		great		came	
new		just		man		line		follow	
only		me		much		mean		form	
place		most		say		old		set	
sound		name		sentence		right		show	
take		our		think		same		small	
work		thing		through		tell		three	
year		very		where		too		want	

Set 16		Set 17		Set 18		Set 19		Set 20	
next		ask		again		air		answer	
another		because		change		animal		every	
big		here		different		away		found	
does		land		hand		house		high	
even		men		home		letter		learn	
large		need		kind		off		mother	
must		read		move		page		should	
put		turn		picture		play		still	
such		went		try		point		study	
well		why		us		spell		world	

From: *Spotlight on Spelling*, Routledge © Glynis Hannell 2009

Activity 20

Commonly used words

LEVEL 3

Set 21		**Set 22**	**Set 23**		**Set 24**		**Set 25**	
add		city	along		always		both	
below		earth	don't		begin		got	
between		eye	few		close		group	
country		father	head		example		important	
food		keep	left		hard		often	
last		light	might		life		paper	
near		never	saw		nest		run	
own		start	story		open		those	
plant		thought	under		seem		together	
school		tree	while		something		until	

Set 26		**Set 27**	**Set 28**		**Set 29**		**Set 30**	
began		book	eat		above		bird	
car		carry	enough		almost		body	
children		four	face		cut		colour	
feet		grow	far		girl		family	
mile		hear	idea		let		leave	
night		once	late		mountain		list	
sea		river	miss		real		music	
side		state	second		money		song	
walk		stop	watch		talk		soon	
white		took	without		young		usual	

Activity 21: Spelling tricks

Teaching notes

In *Spelling tricks* your pupils can try out different ways of learning to spell children's names. The aim of the activity is to make sure that all your pupils have direct experience of the strategies that they can use when they are learning to spell a new word.

Read out each name from the list and ask your pupils to try out two or three of the learning strategies. Make sure that you try each strategy several times. Talk to the pupils about trying different ways of learning for different words.

It is important to encourage your pupils to transfer the strategies they practise here to other words that they learn to spell in the classroom at other times.

The following teacher's chart summarises the various strategies.

What you should ask the pupils to do	Teaching notes
1 • Look at the word carefully. • Say the letters. • Cover the word up and then write it down. • Check you have written it correctly.	This helps the pupil to transfer a visual image into a spoken one (the letters said aloud) and a written one.
2 • Sound the name out and then write the sounds down. • Say the sounds as you write the letters down.	If words are regular then repeatedly *sounding out* and *writing down* is a very good way to learn how to spell the word.
3 • Think of other words with the same spelling pattern.	Working with word 'families' helps to cement spelling patterns, for example *back, Jack, sack, pack*.
4 • Write the name on a *big* piece of paper, with *big* letters. • With coloured pencils write over the word again and again, to make a rainbow-coloured word. • Say the letters as you write.	This is a good method to develop a physical (motor) memory of the word. Saying the letters at the same time enhances learning.
5 • Say if there are there any surprises in how the word is spelt.	Talking about odd patterns, such as *Sean* not rhyming with *mean, bean, lean*, helps the spelling to be remembered.
6 • Find any special patterns of letters.	Noticing patterns in words, such as *Hannah* (same backwards and forwards) or the double letters in *William*, helps with remembering.
7 • Find a trick way to remember how to spell the word.	*Mnemonics* can help with especially difficult words, for example *Put 'jam' in Benjamin*.
8 • 'Ghost-write' the word with a fingertip on the desk with eyes closed.	Tracing the letter sequence helps to build a physical (motor) memory of the spelling.
9 • Close your eyes and see the name in your head.	Some (but not all) pupils can visualise a spelling pattern. This can be teamed with ghost-writing.
10 • Let's all talk about which method of learning you like best. • Say which word was the hardest one on your list. Why was it the hardest? • Say which word was the easiest word. Why was it easy?	It is important for pupils to realise that there is a range of strategies that they can use to learn to spell words. Most pupils will need to use a combination of approaches to get the best result.

Activity 21

LEVEL 1

Spelling tricks

Words to learn

1 Alex

2 Ella

3 Sean

4 Hannah

5 Jack

6 Sarah

7 Sam

8 Lucy

9 Jordan

Your teacher will ask you to try out different ways to learn to spell these names. Which way did you like the best?

Write the boys' and girls' names down in the correct box

Girls' names	Boys' names
_____	_____
_____	_____
_____	_____
_____	_____
_____	_____
_____	_____

Activity 21

Spelling tricks

LEVEL 2

Words to learn

1 Thomas
2 Sophie
3 Daniel
4 Molly
5 Ashley
6 William
7 Jasmine
8 Joseph
9 Leah

Your teacher will ask you to try out different ways to learn to spell these names. Which way did you like the best?

Write the boys' and girls' names down in the correct box

Girls' names	Boys' names
_____	_____
_____	_____
_____	_____
_____	_____
_____	_____
_____	_____
_____	_____

From: *Spotlight on Spelling*, Routledge © Glynis Hannell 2009

Activity 21

Spelling tricks

Words to learn

1 Lauren
2 Stephanie
3 Nathaniel
4 Makayla
5 Benjamin
6 Abigail
7 Christian
8 Charlotte
9 Michael

Your teacher will ask you to try out different ways to learn to spell these names. Which way did you like the best?

Write the boys' and girls' names down in the correct box

Girls' names	Boys' names
_____	_____
_____	_____
_____	_____
_____	_____
_____	_____
_____	_____
_____	_____

Activity 22: Anagrams

Teaching notes

In *Anagrams* pupils are asked to make as many words as they can, using the letters of the word provided. The purpose of this is to develop the pupils' ability to manipulate letters to create spelling patterns, and to generalise from one spelling to another: '*I can make "had", so can I also make "bad"?*'

This activity stretches every pupil's spelling skills, by forcing them to approach spelling from another direction. Instead of asking themselves '*What letters do I need to spell this word?*', they are forced to ask themselves '*What words can I spell with these letters?*'

For pupils who find this task difficult, the teacher can provide extra scaffolding. For example, the teacher may:

- give the pupil letters to start their words, for example '*Let's use "ha" from "birthday" to start some words*';
- give clues to possible words, for example '*Think of a word that is the opposite of young*';
- provide plastic letters to make the whole word and then manipulate to make other words;
- ask questions such as '*Can you make the word "ape" from pancake?*';
- model strategies to find the words, such as taking one letter at a time as an initial letter, or finding commonly used letter pairs such as *sh, sh, oa, ay, at* or *en*.

There are many, many smaller words that can be made from the words given. A sample of possibilities is given below.

Level 1

goldfish	old, gold, fish, dog, dig, lid, hid, log, fog, hog, fig, oil, slid, slog, fold, hold, fold, sold, god, golf, dish, his	**postman**	post, man, pot, not, son, pan, top, map, mop, stop, spot, spat, snap, oat, most, mat, pat, sat, ant, stamp
birthday	birth, day, hat, rat, bat, hit, bit, ray, hay, bay, rib, bit, bad, art, try, had, hid, bid, rid, bath, bird, hard, hair, third	**peanut**	pea, nut, pan, pat, pen, pet, put, tap, tea, ten, ape, ant, tune, pant, tuna, neat, aunt
pancake	pan, can, cap, nap, pen, pea, pack, neck, peak, cake, cane, cape, ape	**carport**	car, port, tap, rat, cat, pat, cot, rot, pot, rap, cap, part, cart, oar, roar, port, parrot
teacher	the, he, her, tea, rat, hat, cat, car, art, tree, teach, chat, cart, hate, heat, three	**spaceman**	space, man, pen, pan, can, map, cap, nap, sap, ape, pea, camp, came, name, same
shopping	pig, pin, pop, hop, hopping, his, hog, sip, hip, pip, ship, nip, spin, song, hippo, shop, posh		

Level 2

elephant	the, tap, pen, hen, ten, pat, then, tale, tape, path, peel, lane, late, leap, pale, help, heat, plate, plant, petal, halt	**helicopter**	the, rip, oil, hit, tip, rot, hot, ice, tile, toil, poet, hole, toe, lip, hop, cot, rice, pile, hero, echo, coil, pilot, topic
doughnut	tug, go, on, do, nut, not, hut, hug, got, gun, god, hog, hot, thug, thud, hunt, tough, hound	**astronaut**	art, ant, at, us, nut, tan, sat, stun, roast, torn, star, rat, turn, aunt, strut, trot, tour, trust
children	rid, child, die, din, hen, her, nice, rice, rich, ride, rind, line, ice, lend, hire, herd, inch, hide, dice	**caterpillar**	cat, pill, pillar, tar, tap, rat, pie, ill, let, lip, trap, trip, ace, tall, tape, ripe, real, reap, race, late, lace, clip, clap, trial, racer
because	be, cause, sea, see, sue, bus, bee, ace, use, scab, ease, cub, case, cab, base, scuba, sauce, cubes, cease	**television**	toe, vet, ten, set, see, son, not, one, eve, vote, vein, veil, tile, oven, sent, nose, lost, lion, evil, visit, steel, love
snowball	snow, ball, bow, ban, owl, sob, own, swan, wall, slow, blow, loan, also, lawn, sawn		

Level 3

underpants	under, pants, sun, net, pet, pan, pea, sea, sad, turn, spun, tune, tape, read, past, dune, peanut, parent, depart	**nightmare**	night, mare, tag, tan, the, tie, mat, hen, term, team, train, rate, neat, name, mint, earn, earth, anger, magnet
breakfast	break, fast, eat, east, beak, brake, after, baker, basket, freak, bark, stare, base, fear, feast, safe, bear, beast	**September**	pet, set, bee, tree, term, step, stem, teem, seem, seep, pest, steep, reset, metre, peter, ember, temper, pester
hamburger	ham, gum, bug, hug, ear, arm, grab, are, bag, beam, bear, argue, amber, barge	**thousand**	out, ton, son, nut, oat, hat, hot, ant, ash, undo, and, toad, stun, host, hound, haunt, shout, hand
drainpipe	drain, pipe, ran, pip, pie, rid, pin, are, ape, dip, ear, end, ripe, ride, read, pain, paid, pair, dear, pear, near, dare	**alligator**	all, log, oar, tag, oat, rag, got, ill, trio, tall, tail, toil, riot, oral, liar, goat, troll, ratio, rail, grill, gorilla
together	to, get, her, rot, toe, get, got, her, hoe, hog, hot, trot, ego, tree, here, hero, teeth, there, three, other, greet, hotter		

Activity 22

Anagrams

LEVEL 1

How many new words can you make from these words?

1 goldfish _____

_____

2 birthday _____

_____

3 pancake _____

_____

4 teacher _____

_____

5 shopping _____

_____

6 postman _____

_____

7 peanut _____

_____

8 carport _____

_____

9 spaceman _____

_____

From: *Spotlight on Spelling*, Routledge © Glynis Hannell 2009

Activity 22

Anagrams

LEVEL 2

How many new words can you make from
these words?

1   elephant   _____

_____

2   doughnut   _____

_____

3   children   _____

_____

4   because   _____

_____

5   snowball   _____

_____

6   helicopter   _____

_____

7   astronaut   _____

_____

8   caterpillar   _____

_____

9   television   _____

_____

Activity 22

Anagrams

LEVEL 3

How many new words can you make from
these words?

1 underpants

_____

_____

2 breakfast

_____

_____

3 hamburger

_____

_____

4 drainpipe

_____

_____

5 together

_____

_____

6 nightmare

_____

_____

7 September

_____

_____

8 thousand

_____

_____

9 alligator

_____

_____

From: *Spotlight on Spelling*, Routledge © Glynis Hannell 2009

Activity 23: Twisters

Teaching notes

This activity is a written version of tongue twisters. Indeed, as the teacher, you will find that several of the items need very careful pronunciation to avoid making mistakes! For example, sentences such as *Did the crab grab the bag?* or *Sue saw Sally singing in thick silk socks* are not that easy to say correctly. However, this makes *Twisters* fun for everyone.

Dictation

The sentences can be used as dictation exercises and will really stretch the pupils' listening and spelling skills.

Copying

Pupils can also just copy the sentences to see how the words work out, with rhymes, alliteration, odd spelling patterns and some quirky ideas.

Discussion

The sentences can also be used as discussion topics. You can ask your pupils to be detectives, looking at each sentence to spot what is unusual about the pattern of spellings, for example:

• **Alliteration**
In some sentences alliteration is used, as almost all the words share the same initial letter, as in *Dad dug the dog a deep den*, or *Horrible Horace hated hearing hedgehogs howling.*

• **Rhymes with the same spelling**
In other sentences rhymes are used, and it is useful for your pupils to notice how often the same spelling pattern occurs in sentences such as *Fred sped on his sled*, or *Nice mice like spice with rice.*

• **Rhymes with different spelling patterns**
These can be really challenging, for example *honey* rhymes with *bunny* and *fox* rhymes with *socks.* Ask your pupils to spot the words that have rhymes but that do not look the same.

• **Same sound, different spelling**
There are several examples of the same sound being spelt differently, for example *Perfect Percy* has a *purple purse*, and the old favourite *I scream* and *ice cream.*

• **Tricky spellings**
Some words in these sentences have tricky spellings, such as *Do giant gnomes have giant combs?*, or *Clarry the cat caught a cold. Cough drops cured him, so I am told.*

There are no teacher's charts for this activity.

Activity 23

Twisters

LEVEL 1

<u>Listen carefully</u> to your teacher, who will tell you what to do.

1   Six snails sang sad songs.

2   Dad dug the dog a deep den.

3   It's funny my bunny likes honey.

4   Goldfish are cold fish.

5   Can a fox wear socks and frocks?

6   Fred sped on his sled.

7   The bat, the rat and the big fat cat all sat on grandpa's hat.

8   Nice mice like spice with rice.

9   Did the crab grab the bag?

Activity 23

Twisters

LEVEL 2

<u>Listen carefully</u> to your teacher, who will tell you what to do.

1 I scream for ice cream.

2 Brian the bear braved the bites of a billion bees.

3 Do poodles eat oodles of noodles?

4 I suppose my nose can reach my toes.

5 Do giant gnomes have giant combs?

6 Picky people mutter while eating peanut butter.

7 Six silly sheep saw six shepherds sleeping.

8 Do your bananas wear pyjamas?

9 Sue saw Sally singing in thick silk socks.

Activity 23

Twisters

LEVEL 3

<u>Listen carefully</u> to your teacher, who will tell you what to do.

1 Grapes grow gradually greener in Greece.

2 Father put a fatter feather in his leather hat.

3 Six selfish shellfish shiver in the shallows.

4 Horrible Horace hated hearing hedgehogs howling.

5 Perfect Percy's purple purse was full of precious pebbles.

6 Clarry the cat caught a cold. Cough drops cured him, so I am told.

7 Camels with cameras go camping in caravans.

8 Do you whistle when a bristle or a thistle pricks your thumb?

9 Six singing swans swam swiftly in the swamp.

From: *Spotlight on Spelling*, Routledge © Glynis Hannell 2009

Activity 24: Learn your own words

Teaching notes

Note: *Learn your own words* is best suited to pupils who find spelling reasonably easy. *Seven in a row* (Activity 25), which follows, is more suited to pupils who find spelling particularly difficult.

Irregular words that are not yet in the pupil's repertoire of spelling will need to be deliberately taught and practised, until the correct spelling becomes automatic.

Every pupil will be working at their own level. One pupil may be learning to spell *the*, while another pupil may be learning *although*.

Because this is an individual activity, no levels are given. The worksheet can, of course, be used as many times as required, with new words entered on a fresh sheet as necessary.

The steps in this activity are:

• *Step 1*
The pupil (with the teacher's help) finds three irregular words that they cannot spell. These are entered in the top row of the chart, ready to be learnt.

• *Step 2*
The pupil looks at the word and learns it 'their way'. This can be by reciting the letters, rainbow writing (writing over a large version of the word with different colours), tracing the word on the desk with a fingertip,

thinking and talking about the spelling pattern, imagining the word with eyes closed, writing the word on scrap paper or whatever method the pupil finds most effective. The teacher will be important in guiding the individual pupil to find the best mix of learning methods that works for them.

• *Step 3*
The pupil covers the first two rows of the chart and writes the word from memory.

• *Step 4*
The pupil checks the word to see if the spelling is correct.

• *Step 5*
Whether the word was correct or not before, the pupil writes the word down again.

• *Steps 6, 7 and 8*
The pupil continues to cover, write and check.

For some pupils this activity is sufficient to reinforce the spelling pattern of irregular words. However, for pupils who find spelling difficult, this may not be enough to teach the spelling of the word for long-term recall. In this case, it is suggested that teachers move on to the next, more intensive activity, *Seven in a row* (Activity 25).

Activity 24

Learn your own words

ALL LEVELS

		Word 1	Word 2	Word 3
1	Write the word			
2	Look at the word and learn it your way			
3	Cover the word Write the word			
4	Check			
5	Cover the word Write the word			
6	Check			
7	Cover the word Write the word			
8	Check			

From: *Spotlight on Spelling*, Routledge © Glynis Hannell 2009

Activity 25: Seven in a row

Teaching notes

Note: *Seven in a row* is best suited to pupils who find spelling difficult.

In *Learn your own words* (Activity 24) pupils were asked to learn a word and then write it from memory three times in quick succession. This works well when the pupil finds learning to spell reasonably easy, but is often insufficient for pupils who find retention of spelling patterns more difficult.

In *Seven in a row* pupils who find it difficult to 'hold' a spelling pattern practise the same word time and time again, on separate occasions, until they can successfully spell the word seven times in a row. This really helps the pupils to master the word fully. Teachers can individualise this activity by changing the number of correct attempts required to complete the task. Seven has been found to be a good number for solid learning for most pupils, but individual pupils may be better suited to *Five in a row* or *Ten in a row*, or whatever the teacher finds works best.

At the start of the activity the teacher has one or more blank word cards (photocopied from the next page). The teacher will judge if the pupil can cope with several cards at once or whether it will be better to work on one word at a time.

The pupil and teacher select a word that the pupil has found difficult to spell correctly. The word is written clearly on the blank portion of the card. The teacher introduces the spelling to the pupil. They may use *Learn your own words* (Activity 24) as an introduction, or the teacher may prefer to teach by other methods, such as those introduced in *Spelling tricks* (Activity 21).

The pupil's ability to spell the word is checked regularly and the date recorded on the card. Each time the pupil makes a mistake, additional teaching and supervised practice is provided, in preparation for the next checkpoint. Every checkpoint must be at least one day after the previous one. Once the pupil has seven consecutive ticks, the word is considered to be well and truly learnt and a new word is chosen.

Below is a sample of a completed *Seven in a row* card.

eyes	Date 21/4	Date 22/4	Date 23/4	Date 24/4	Date 25/4
	✓	✗	✓	✓	✓
	Date 28/4	Date 30/4	Date 2/5	Date 5/5	Date 6/5
	✓	✓	✗	✓	✓
	Date 8/5	Date 12/5	Date 15/5	Date 17/5	Date 19/5
	✓	✓	✓	✓	✓ *Well done!*
	Date	Date	Date	Date	Date

Activity 25

Seven in a row

ALL LEVELS

	Date	Date	Date	Date	Date
	Date	Date	Date	Date	Date
	Date	Date	Date	Date	Date
	Date	Date	Date	Date	Date

	Date	Date	Date	Date	Date
	Date	Date	Date	Date	Date
	Date	Date	Date	Date	Date
	Date	Date	Date	Date	Date